Sis. Hannah,

Our Sunday Scha ~~~~~~~~~ such a blessing for us both & We
Pray that our Heavenly Father will guide
your walk to the kingdom & keep
you steadfast in Love & faith until
then!

    With Love & Brotherly Support

    Bro. Eric & Brian

Speaking to the Heart

Speaking to the Heart

Dennis Gillett

The Christadelphian
404 Shaftmoor Lane, Hall Green, Birmingham B28 8SZ, UK

2015

First published 2015

© 2015 The Christadelphian Magazine and Publishing Association

ISBN 978 0 85189 321 1 (print edition)
ISBN 978 0 85189 322 8 (electronic edition)

Printed and bound in Malta by
Gutenberg Press Limited

Contents

Foreword

R EADING through what follows in these pages, I am moved to a measure of sadness for those readers who are under thirty years of age. Such never heard that Banbury accent, never saw the confidential manner of this brother on the platform, never heard his so appropriate stories which memorably illuminated what he had to say. He was not a 'speaking brother' in the general manner of speaking brethren, he was unique in that he was above all an ardent preacher. Every word he spoke brought new light into the Gospel message.

When he fell asleep in 1992, his widow Sister Ruth rang to tell me that she had a collection of shoeboxes upstairs in the wardrobe. But these were no ordinary shoeboxes for they contained the vast majority of her husband's talks. Here was a man who typed out in full everything he said to his congregations. Yet those congregations would never have known that as he spoke. I once asked his daughter Sister Lois what book her father used beyond the scriptures for his preparation. A good thesaurus was her immediate reply – and doesn't that show in what you have heard or read from Brother Dennis!

Many of you will have read and greatly benefited from the books which were published by the CMPA as a result of that shoebox find. This particular collection has come from various sources. The chapters on Prayer have been compiled from a number of overlapping notes which were given as exhortations, studies and fraternal addresses. Some are over sixty years old, yet are just as refreshing as when first given. The Deuteronomy

Studies were originally given at The Oxford Conference in 1973 and repeated in South Africa. "Matthew's Messiah" was given at the Midwest Bible School in the United States in 1984. Brother Dennis emphasises that "personal reformation is required in preparation for the kingdom of heaven". It couldn't have been put more succinctly, could it? Despite their age, these addresses come to life on the printed page for subsequent generations of brethren and sisters to be cheered and uplifted while we wait for the coming of the King.

I trust you will forgive a purposeful misquotation from scripture – "Never man *wrote* like this man". Brother Dennis had the ability to make one eager to turn to the next page to read what he has to say there. His own comment upon quoting from Isaiah 11 says it all about this man of God – "Many a weary head rested upon these words of comfort. Many a broken spirit found healing there. Many a fearful and frightened soul took courage through these promises ..."

May you all gain as much strength, encouragement and uplifting joy from the words of this godly man as I have done since I first met him in 1953.

Trevor A. Pritchard
Coventry
November 2015

BOOK ONE
Discipleship in Deuteronomy

1 |

Remember the way

I MUST explain to you that this first section on discipleship in Deuteronomy has a rather long introduction. The reason is, that in order to appreciate the idea that these studies are intended to convey, you need to grasp the principles upon which they are based and the introduction is concerned with trying to expose what those principles are. I say this so that you will not be discouraged right at the beginning. I shall therefore depend on your optimistic fortitude while I go through the introduction.

Relevant and valuable
If you are well taught in the word of God it will come as no surprise to you that the book of Deuteronomy is relevant and is valuable and is altogether helpful in respect of our own discipleship. It is rich in those things which concern our life in Christ Jesus. That is because the master life, which was once revealed and incarnated in the Man of Nazareth, had its roots deep in the principles of the book of Deuteronomy. You will remember that when our Lord was tempted in the wilderness, when he was assaulted by the powers of darkness, in that moment he sought and found his defence in the last words of Moses which were spoken to the people of Israel on the plains of Moab. So that, if proof were needed that this book of Deuteronomy is valuable to his disciples in these days, would be proof enough.

But there are other reasons why the teaching of Deuteronomy is so applicable to ourselves. The words were spoken to the people of God on the threshold of a new life –

on the perimeter of a new land. They were a people who had experienced the hazards and the wonders of the wilderness journey, being led and nurtured by Yahweh their God. They were deeply conscious of their appalling weakness and of their real condition apart from Him.

So I need hardly draw the parallel at this stage – we have good reason to believe that the kingdom of God is at hand. I know that some of you are eager with anticipation, prepared with your spiritual hats and coats on, just waiting for the day of possession. That's not a complaint – I'm glad that it's true. We are right to sing as we do, "Remember the glory, remember the land".

Then in addition there is something else to ponder. Some of the things which Moses spoke are so fundamental that they are perpetually true. They are true on every level of life; they are timeless in their application. They are true because he spoke on the basis of unchanging principles. That is why this book is so valuable. The principles are eternal – they were true then, they are true now. So the introduction is seeking to prove that to you. The introduction is seeking to show you that this is so. These are words spoken so long ago in what may seem to us a far-off land, but they are utterly true today wherever we are.

Let me, therefore, in this introduction illustrate what I mean. I want to bring you to look in depth at Deuteronomy 29:29:

"The secret things belong unto the LORD our God: but those things which are revealed belong unto us and to our children for ever, that we may do all the words of this law."

Now we want to look at those words on three distinct levels. First of all we shall view them in their immediate context in the life of Israel. Then we shall see them as part of the life of humanity on the ordinary level. Finally we shall look at them as a principle of life for those who are elect according to the foreknowledge of God, called, blood-sprinkled and chosen, such as those in Christ are.

Let us then examine those words, first of all in the context of the life of Israel. Let us notice the order of the process that

Moses is describing here. It is ordered in the way God saw it – it is the process in the sight of God.

First there are the secret things known only to God. Then in the course of His purpose He reveals part of those secret things to men, that is to say, His word is spoken and His will is subsequently documented. The result is that men are able to respond to it, and as a result of it, they are able to keep His law. So that is the process – the secret things of God are revealed by God, understood by men, responded to by men, who then are in a position to keep His law. Now that is God's view of the condition that Moses describes.

Man's view of it is different. In fact, man's view of it, in a way, is exactly opposite – it is reversed. For men, first of all there is the revelation from God. Now apart from that revelation there is nothing that we could know of God really – and certainly not of His purpose. But, as a result of the revelation, men are able to respond and may keep His law, and as a result of keeping His law, they discover the secret things. You see that in the sight of God the process begins with the secret things, whereas in the sight of men it ends with the secret things. It is a reversal.

Now our business is to examine the process from man's point of view. There are three elements – the secret things, the revealed things and the capacity to keep the law.

The life of Israel

Let's think then of the revealed things in relation to the people of Israel. We could say that the revealed things are all those signs and signals that came from God to His people right from their deliverance in Egypt. These revelations continued during their wanderings as part of their protection by God. So they came to know what God was really like, and came to know themselves in the process.

That is what we could say, but there is a strange verse in Deuteronomy 29 which I would like you to notice: it is verse 4. Every word in the Bible is important so let us note the words carefully:

"Yet the LORD hath not given you an heart to perceive, and eyes to see, and ears to hear, unto this day."

That's a strange sentence. It seems to say that in their wanderings and in their wilderness experience, blindness in part had happened to Israel. It seems as though God's revelation of Himself had not altogether touched their hearts – it had not altogether penetrated their minds. But now, you see, there is a change. As Moses spoke these last words to Israel on the plains of Moab in this great discourse we call the book of Deuteronomy, it seems now that their hearts are equipped to know, their eyes are able to see, their ears can hear: the things which hitherto had been hidden in a sense, the secret things, are now being revealed. That is to say, there is a limitation put on the period of Israel's indifference. "Unto this day" means that the days of blindness are coming to an end – that there is a sense that from now on the knowable will be known, the unseeable will be seen, the inaudible will be heard, the revealed things "which belong unto us and to our children" are to be understood.

What were the revealed things? Well they are the things of which Moses spoke: the reiteration, the development of the great law first spoken at Sinai, then enlarged and expanded. When you read this great law carefully, it is quite evident that it is not by any means just a set of rules. It is, essentially, a way of life. It is a way of life which touches the people of God in every aspect of their living, and in every recess of their experience.

How wrong it is to say that all law is in the Old Testament and all grace is in the New Testament. This law of God spoken by Moses is rich in grace. It reveals God as a loving Father caring deeply for the salvation of His people. Compassion is the golden thread which runs through the fabric of the law. Mercy is the quality of its directions, love is the master passion of its provisions.

Just think quickly of some examples. Think of the great idea of sanctuary in the Law of Moses, the provision of cities of refuge for those who would need protection from the hate and the harm of those who would hastily seek to take revenge.

Or think of the man who was called to go to war and he has just married his young wife. You know, the laws of what we call civilised counties will call him nevertheless, whether he was just married or not – it makes no difference. They will separate him from his wife, be he ever so young. But *this* ancient law, divine in its provision, divinely compassionate, said, 'No'. He must stay and realise the joy of life for life and love for love which God had bestowed upon him in his marriage.

Then think of the fear of the man who, being afraid, is forced to go to the battle; the faint-hearted who is forced to fight. The compassion of the law made provision for such and provided a way of release.

The poor were never to be exploited, the rich were always to be merciful, there had to be just weights and just measures – these things had to be established. There is purity, and justice and mercy, and righteousness, and holiness, and there is joy in obedience. So Israel, in living this way of life, would discover what their God was really like. By submission to the revealed things, the secret things of God may be discovered.

This then was the master principle which Moses enunciated in his last words to the people of God as they were going forward into the new experience of life.

Ordinary human experience

Well, we can leave that local situation now and try to think of the great principle on the level of ordinary human experience as part of the science of life. Remember what the principle is – I hope I won't weary you by keep saying what it is. I don't want you to lose sight of it:

> "The secret things belong unto the LORD our God: but those things which are revealed belong unto us and to our children for ever, that we may do all the words of this law."

Now let us think of those words as part of the science of daily life. First of all there are the secret things which belong to God, then there are the revealed things which men might discover. As a result of submission to those revealed things, they are able to understand the secret things. As they keep the law, so they come nearer to the truth.

Now for myself, I believe that it is a divinely natural part of men to seek to know what is unknown. You may not agree, but this is how it appears to me. It is part of human nature; it is part of man's make-up. God made him like this. It is one of the things which distinguishes him from all other created things. It is the thing that places him at the summit of divine creation.

There is in the mind of man a note of perpetual interrogation. I believe this to be a proper part of God's purpose, so when somebody comes to me and says, "Brother Gillett, do you not think it is a terrible thing for men to reach the moon?", I say, "I do not". I am not shocked. In all honesty I must say that it is what I would have expected them to do because they are like this. Within certain bounds it is a perfectly proper activity set deep in human nature. Now I am very careful to say "within certain bounds" because it is evident that there are certain secret things which men may not know and when they reach that point it marks the limit of their investigation. Beyond that, God will not allow them to go. When man reaches that limit, God will halt him, and for the time being he must be halted. He must accept the mystery.

I happen to believe that every discovery of man is a revelation of God – that is to say, men discover what God is ready to allow them to know at a set time, according to His purpose. I believe that when Peter said of the King, "He is Lord of all", he meant that. Every word in the Bible is important. He *is* Lord of all: Lord of the scientist, Lord of the architect, Lord of the physicist, Lord of the politician – they may not recognise him as Lord, but he is.

Nevertheless, enquiring men only discover what God is disposed to reveal. So, it is no coincidence that when the time was right for the great spiritual reformation in Europe, Gutenberg developed the printing press. It is just as certain that there is no coincidence in that as the world draws nearer to the final agony, men have discovered nuclear energy.

Now here you see the vital thing to observe – behind every revealed thing, there is a hidden thing. Behind every visible thing there is the invisible thing. The literal meaning of the Hebrew word for 'revealed things' is 'the things which are denuded'. If you want to go to the literal Hebrew, it may not be so poetic, but never mind: the things which are denuded, that is, the things which are stripped are things that can be touched and appreciated by the senses. On the other hand, the literal meaning of the Hebrew word for the 'secret things' is just the opposite. It means the 'clothed things'; the things which are covered – things which are real enough, but they are hidden by a covering, so that they cannot be seen and they cannot be touched and they cannot be felt. There is no doubt of their reality, but they are hidden. Now I am saying that behind every revealed thing there is a hidden thing. Behind the material, always there is the invisible.

And this is true of every level of existence – on the level of the material, on the level of the mental, and on the level of the spiritual. Let me just give you a very simple example – a glass of water. Behind this glass of water, first of all there is the designer. There is the skill of the maker. There is the idea of the craftsman. And there is the love of the kind hands of the one who was thoughtful enough to provide it for the thirsty so he could be refreshed. And so it is with life. Behind the great poem, the symphony, the philosophy – there is the invisible mind of the poet, the composer, the philosopher. Now this great principle is true in the realm of the spiritual. Behind the outward things of religion there are the spiritual counterparts. There are the outward and visible works of the religious life but behind them we know that it is the invisible and spiritual motive that is the reality.

We may sing songs today, and the songs will be heard, but you know that it is the condition of your hearts that will make this an act of worship. If the condition of your heart is wrong, the song will go no higher than the roof.

Baptism is of vital importance, but we know that the outward act of getting wet in a bath is really of no consequence.

What makes it important is the act of submission. The outward act must be matched by the invisible grace of the right quality – the act of faith. The point is that the revealed thing, the external thing, and the hidden thing, the invisible thing, are closely united. One is the counterpart of the other. The revealed thing expresses as much of the hidden thing as we by our consciousness are able to understand at any given time.

The master principle, therefore, is this – discover a law which is revealed in the revealed thing, and you have found the method by which the secret thing may be discovered. Obey the law which you discover, and you have the possibility of entering into communion with the secret things of God – the hidden things.

Can I just give you a couple of illustrations? Take electricity. Once (measured by human time) long ago men were probing, they were watching, they were pondering. Accidentally at first something pressed upon the imagination of the watcher. What did the watcher do? Well he set himself to discover the law which he suspected must operate behind the revelation that he discovered. He went on patiently, and going on patiently he discovered the law, and when he obeyed the law he found himself in the midst of forces of which he had never dreamed, of which he had no conception hitherto and which today we take as commonplace.

Take another example – the world of horticulture. Years ago, men watched and saw the growth and habit of a little daisy-like plant they call *compositae*. They investigated it, they tried it, they watched it, they nursed it, they noticed its habits, they discovered the law that was in it, they unclothed the secret of its growth and its possibility. Today it is a marvel, a joy, a flame of glory which they call 'chrysanthemum'.

Obey the law of the revealed thing, and immediately, I tell you, you have touched the infinite force within it. Do you know that there is a law within all created things? You take, for example, the glory of the tulip. The glory of the tulip is that it obeys the law that is within it and upon it. Being faithful to that law it exposes the secret things which are locked within the mystery of what we call a tulip bulb. It gives God glory because it is faithful to the law of the tulip which is locked within it. And it exposes the glory of God because of its faithfulness.

Now, nevertheless, although the secret things are exposed in this realm of things, are they not to us still secret? Do you not feel this in your heart? We may come to observe the revealed things and yet in some ways they are still secret. Take the mystery of the tulip. Is it not to the botanist still a mystery? Do you know, for example, how it is there is perfume in a violet? Have you ever thought of it? It never ceases while it lives. From whence does it come? It is always there. It is always scenting the air. From whence does it come? – it is ever present.

Or again, by what strange alchemy of things is this petal red and this petal yellow? Is it not a mystery? They tell me that diamonds are made of carbon and so is a jellyfish. If you understand that, well you are welcome to it!

It makes me smile when I hear men say they cannot believe in the resurrection because it asks them to accept a mystery. You know, we live and move and have our being right in the heart of mystery. We are surrounded by it. And the great crowning principle of Moses is marked for us there in this great book of Deuteronomy. "The secret things belong unto the LORD our God: but those things which are revealed belong unto us and to our children for ever, that we may do all the words of this law."

Discover the revealed things, find the law that is in them, obey the law, and you will uncover the secret forces which hitherto are hidden. Perchance in doing it on the level of ordinary life, the men who discovered electricity, or developed *compositae*, found themselves co-workers with God, found themselves close to the mystery of life, developers of His creation, the revelation of His glory.

Remember, the things seen are only the externals of some deeper thing. Our Lord made use of external things but he never led us to believe that the figure was really the fact. When he said, "I am the true vine", for example, he didn't mean he was borrowing the vine as a figure of what he was like. As it appears to me, the deeper truth is that Jesus is the original vine, living and bearing fruit, being crushed and offering his blood, the flowing out of him of life and restoration for men. And then, God, as it were, granted the vine in the field as a replica of what His Son was like – Christ is the true vine. He didn't mean that all other vines are false. This is not a case of 'true' and 'false', this is 'original' and 'replica'. He is the original vine – all other vines are replicas.

When we handle the common loaf we say, 'This is bread', but that isn't the whole truth. The common loaf in a sense is a symbol of the true bread. Thereafter there is another bread which is the real bread. "I am the living bread which came down from heaven: if any man eat of this bread, he shall live for ever." There is a sense in which every common loaf of bread is a sacramental symbol of the bread of heaven.

The cross was a rough timber construction made in the shape with which we are familiar (if anybody wants to argue it was just a stake, I don't mind). It was a rough piece of wood, one piece lying across another. That also is a revealed thing at the back of which is a secret thing more real and more unfathomable. The real cross is the love of God passing from heaven to earth, and lying across it in red and scarlet is sin.

Behind every visible thing there is a secret thing and Moses said the revealed things are ours and what they are for. They are so we may pursue the revealed things, obey the law which is therein and become possessors of the secret things, things that bring us into touch with God and with the secret things that are associated with Him.

Well now, that was (in case you have forgotten) the application of the principle on the level of ordinary life.

A principle of life for the elect
We have now to think about it, as I said, on the spiritual level, that is to say, in respect of ourselves, and it is to be thought of on the practical level. As you obey His law, and as you incarnate His will in your own life, so as a consequence you draw nearer to

the deep things of God; that is to say, in your experience of His ways, so you uncover the secret things of His will and the true meaning of His word.

Can I bring you back to Deuteronomy chapter 8? Moses said in verse 2:

"And thou shalt remember all the way which the LORD thy God led thee these forty years in the wilderness, to humble thee, and to prove thee, to know what was in thine heart, whether thou wouldest keep his commandments, or no."

First of all observe the mystery and the wonder of God's method. Isn't it strange? He led them circuitously so that at last they would be straight. He delayed them in the wilderness so that at last He might speed them on their way into the good land. And when Moses uses the word "prove", it doesn't mean that God was wanting to find out what was in them, for He knew that already. He wanted them to find out for themselves what they were like. He wanted them to be outwardly what they were inwardly and in the keeping of His law, the secret things were revealed.

You see, all God's methods tend to humbling. He brings His people into circumstances which will reveal the secret forces of their own nature. He brings them into situations which will compel them to recognise that essentially they depend upon Him. If there is secret rebellion, for example, in a man's heart, that man under the providence of God will be led into a situation where the rebellion will be brought into the light because in the light it can be recognised; in the light it can be repudiated, and in the light it can be abandoned for what it is. And so it is with impurity or cowardice or greed. God brings a man into such situations as will bring out of him what he is really like.

A good example of this is the case of Judas Iscariot. They made him the Lord's treasurer. They said about Judas, 'Give him the bag'. Now it could have brought out the best in him if it was there. Being the treasurer could have given him the opportunity to exercise generosity and sympathy and compassion. But instead it revealed him to be dishonest, covetous, and hard. Some men discover the truth about themselves in the winepress of God's purpose. When you are in the Truth, you are, in a sense, in a winepress and God is making you to be outwardly what you are inwardly.

Now if that was all there is to say about it, then indeed it would be a terrible thing to think about in isolation. But there is more to it, and notice again what Moses said in verse 2:

"And thou shalt remember all the way which the LORD thy God led thee."

Now let's mark it well. "Remember all the way." It means that the remembering is a backward look, but is also a look forward in hope. You see, one of the great certainties of life (I wonder if you will be sympathetic with me in this) – one of the great certainties of life is in the past. Of course, it can be one of the great agonies too. For some of us, the past is an agony. It's irreparable; it can't be changed. But nevertheless, it says 'certainty'. That is why it is certain – it cannot be changed.

Now when these words were first uttered, it was for the people of God a time of change. The wilderness was before them, the new life was ahead, the new year was beginning with them, a new era with its new responsibilities – the responsibilities of anticipation. These people were on the fringe of a new life and a new land. They knew something of the country which was before them; indeed the words of Moses had told them in one of the finest pieces of poetry in the whole of the Bible. Did you notice it in chapter 8?

"For the LORD thy God bringeth thee into a good land, a land of brooks of water, of fountains and depths that spring out of valleys and hills; a land of wheat, and barley, and vines, and fig trees, and pomegranates; a land of oil olive, and honey; a land wherein thou shalt eat bread without scarceness, thou shalt not lack any thing in it; a land whose stones are iron, and out of whose hills thou mayest dig brass. When thou hast eaten and art full, then thou shalt bless the LORD thy God for the good land which he hath given thee."   (verses 7-10)

They knew something of the land into which they were going, but they didn't know what lay between them and the good land.

So that a little later on Joshua is going to say to them, "Ye have not passed this way heretofore" (Joshua 3:4). They were aware therefore of the uncertainty of the future.

Now there may be a certain fascination in facing the unknown, but often with the fascination there is the fear. There are the anxieties which arise, doubts whether we shall be able to meet all the things that lie ahead. So we must mark the fascination and the fear and consider this – that for the wise man there is value in both. In verse 5 of Joshua chapter 3 he said:

"Sanctify yourselves: for tomorrow the LORD will do wonders among you."

Now what he meant was, 'Tomorrow is the Lord's, therefore today is for you because you cannot see tomorrow'. In the very uncertainty there is value because it compels men of faith and men of wisdom to grasp the forces which will make them equal to the things of tomorrow. You see, if I am to march among precipices, in the midst of ambush foes, one step at a time, one day at a time, over terrain which is strange and unknown, facing mystery and uncertainty, then sanctified common sense compels me to be equipped and fortified for the journey.

I almost hesitate to make the parallel now at this stage between those people and ourselves, save to say that we do not know what lies between us and the kingdom of God. We know it is near, we thank God it is near, but personally we do not know what lies ahead for us. I do not know how many victorious Jerichos there may be for me. I do not know how many disappointments like Ai there may be.

But you and I ought to be deeply conscious of the responsibilities of anticipation. I think we are entitled – nay we are constrained – to ask, apart from the uncertainty, what are the certainties we may grasp and take with us on the journey.

Well, first of all let us go back and hear the word of Moses as he came into the end of his leadership. As the people turned to face the new circumstances and the new experience, in Deuteronomy 8:2, again he charged them: "Thou shalt remember all the way which the LORD thy God led thee these forty years in the wilderness." I repeat again, therefore, that one of the certainties of life is the past. It is fixed and irreparable as we have said already, and to the man of faith it can be "a covert from the tempest; as rivers of water in a dry place, as the shadow of a great rock in a weary land". Why? Why is the past so valuable? Well, because past deliverance predicts future deliverance; because past succour promises future succour; because past guidance predicates future guidance.

This is what I mean. There is a river before us – how shall it be crossed? Well, measure the problem of the river by the problem of the Red Sea. The water was divided then – it can be divided again. There is an unknown land before us – how shall we find our way? Well, measure the unknown land which is before us by the known wilderness which is behind us. He who led once can lead again. There is a new country. How shall we be sustained in the new country? Well, measure the coming hunger by the past manna and the past water.

This is how David met the problems of the present. When he was assaulted by his enemies, his faith was assaulted and he fell back on his remembrance of the past. It's in Psalm 42; you will remember it well. The enemies of David chided him. They said, "Where is thy God?" They were saying, 'Where is He now?' 'What good is He now?' 'What is He doing for you?' They assaulted his faith. "Why art thou cast down, O my soul?", he said, "And why art thou disquieted in me?" It was an invitation to doubt, an invitation to turn traitor. "Why art thou cast down, O my soul?" And then, in his difficulty, he remembered the past. He said, I remember what this God is like – I remember Jordan and Hermon and Mizar. I remember how He delivered me, He succoured me, He lifted me up, He kept me so that I could sing at last, "Hope thou in God: for I shall yet praise him for the help of his countenance". Remembrance of the past generates hope for the future.

So as you face tomorrow, let nobody take away from you your certainty of yesterday. And of course, there are plenty of people who would like to take it away just as there were in David's day. They may confuse us with the problems of next year, but let them not confuse us about the solutions of life last year. We were led, were we not? You will know what I mean. We were led in the great and terrible wilderness. In the hour of extremity He was there – the great Yahweh.

There was no bread, and it rained from heaven. There was no water, and the flint gushed out. There was no certain way in the dreary wilderness, and He went before us and found a place of rest. We sang a psalm on the same side of the Red Sea. Let nobody frighten you, therefore, with a running river. Never doubt your own experiences. If you know what He is like, this great God of Israel, in the crises and in the commonplaces of life, cling to that at all costs. Think of the day when the bitterest waters were made sweet. Think of the day when you came to Elim at last and rested. Think upon it and make it the inspiration of your life. It is one of the great certainties as we go into the unknown.

I can well believe that there are those who once came to Marah, the place of bitterness. When they experienced Marah, they were nearly broken. And thereafter, they were never the same again. But now, looking back on it, and remembering all the way that the Lord God had led them, they wouldn't be without it, because in the way of Marah, somehow, they discovered the secret things of God. In the way of Marah, they understood better the mystery of His purpose. They came to know more deeply the wonder of His providential care. They were fortified thereby for all the days that lie ahead before at last they enter the good land.

It was in their profound experience of God that they came to realise the deepest meaning of this holy word. In the keeping of His law, His will has been revealed and consequently the secret things have been unveiled because the secret things belong to the Lord our God, but the revealed things belong to us and our children for ever. In the days of past extremity they discovered the riches of His grace. And it is by these things that men live. Do you know this? Not by bread, not by dust, not by roses, roses all the way, not by sunshine, continual sunshine, not even by milk and honey; certainly not by garlic, leeks and onions, not by beautiful rivers – men do not live by these things. Men live by every word that comes from the mouth of God: heard with hushed spirits, obeyed with reverent fear, realised in all the experiences of the way; led out, they are, and led in, obstacles placed in the way, obstacles removed from the way. Today they are being broken, tomorrow they are being remade. Today they are being confined and constricted, tomorrow they are being liberated into new places and new ways. They are being delayed so that they may be speeded on their way. They are being led circuitously so that at last they may go straight. They are being denied so that at last they may be blessed.

How incomprehensible are His ways, how unsearchable His paths – the secret things of God. So at last it is true. The invisible can be seen; the inaudible can be heard; the unknowable can be known. The secret things belong to the Lord our God, but the revealed things belong to us and our children forever, so that we may do all the words of this law and discover the secret things at last.

Now I put it to you with reverence that this process is an essential part of our own discipleship. It is a perpetual inspiration to present endeavour. It is revealed most surely in the great book of Deuteronomy. Amen.

The leading of the eagle

RECALL the idea which these studies seek to follow: that in the book of Deuteronomy there are words of Moses which are so fundamental they have a perpetual relevance to the people of God; that because Moses spoke on the basis of eternal principles, the application is ageless and timeless. What was true then is true now.

The passage we are to ponder now is:

"As an eagle stirreth up her nest, fluttereth over her young, spreadeth abroad her wings, taketh them, beareth them on her wings: so the LORD alone did lead him, and there was no strange god with him." (Deuteronomy 32:11,12)

The first thing to remark is this – that Moses was not only a great prophet, he was also a great poet. It is a strange and wonderful thing that the man who could not speak to Pharaoh because of his stumbling speech could describe the faithfulness of God and the unfaithfulness of His people in such telling and thrilling sentences.

Great poetry

The song of Moses, which as it turned out was the 'swansong' of Moses, is pure poetry. We ought not to miss the point – it is divinely wonderful *poetry*. I know there are some in our community who despise poetry because they say it is unreal and sentimental – but the truth is that often poetry gets to the heart of a matter in a telling and penetrating way, when the use of plain and prosaic language would fail, or at least would not illuminate the issues so clearly.

For example, you could say truthfully of the Messiah that he will provide for and protect his people. But how does Isaiah say it? He is like "a covert from the tempest; as rivers of water in a dry place, as the shadow of a great rock in a weary land" (32:2). Those words have given new hope to all such as are tempest-tossed, parched and heavy laden. They are profound words and they have a profound effect upon all who trust them.

Again it could be said truly of God's people that they will be strengthened and renewed. But how does Isaiah say it? "They shalt mount up with wings as eagles; they shall run, and not be weary; and they shall walk, and not faint" (40:31). Those words are poetry and they stir the emotions, and when the emotions are stirred the will is energised.

The first way of saying it is true but it is cold and without emotion. It is the language of the accountant reading his balance sheet. A man came to me once and said that when he reads his balance sheet it is a very emotional affair – but we must leave that!

The issue is that Isaiah's poetry touches us in our deepest heart. I knew a man in Christ who for twenty years lay paralysed. You can imagine with what hopefulness his soul brooded upon the great words of Isaiah, and pondered his rhetorical method: to begin with the most wonderful thing, mounting up with eagle's wings, and finishing with the most ordinary thing, walking. For that paralysed man, walking would be like mounting up as an eagle. Isaiah's rhetorical method has a special purpose which we must leave now – to return to the issue that by poetry, divinely inspired, the truth of God is magnificently revealed.

And so it is in Deuteronomy 32 – in Moses' song and in those words setting the way of divine government in a figure of the wilderness – the leading of the eagle.

I will say here and now that my knowledge of eagles is limited. They are hard to come upon in north Oxfordshire. Those that I have seen hereabouts are stuffed and mounted in glass cabinets – they have not had anything to eat for forty years! Watching them tells you very little. Most of what I have learned has come from reading – and it agrees with Moses' way of describing their activities.

God leading His people
Notice the words carefully in verses 11 and 12 already quoted. Verse 11 reveals to us the activities of the eagles, but it does not tell us the purpose of the activities. We learn that from verse 12 and the purpose of God. We have to allow the first part of the declaration to be interpreted by the second. Here is a strange thing – the purpose of the eagles is revealed in the declaration about the purpose of God. The eagle is stirring up the nest, hovering over the young. The eagle is spreading abroad his wings, catching them and bearing them on his pinions. Why is the eagle acting thus? In order that he may lead the eaglets – so that they may be taught and guided. It is evident when you take both verses together that the ways of the Lord with His people are revealed by what is said concerning the eagles.

How does God lead His people? He stirs up the nest, He hovers over His own, He spreads His wings before them, He catches them and carries them. This is a revelation of the way of God with His people.

I understand that eaglets have a voracious appetite and when they have been fed they desire sleep. I am not going to suggest that sleep after feeding is something peculiar to eagles. Without being zoological, there are other species with the same habit. But it is a fact that disturbance is the last thing the eaglets want. And it is the very thing upon which the parent eagles insist. The young birds are turned out of the nest, they are compelled to strive for elevation; when they drop they are caught by the father eagle – as they flutter and fall, so they are borne on the pinions of the father bird. The mother bird disturbs and hovers, the father bird swoops and catches the young as they falter.

So let us remark in the poetry of this declaration on the method of God leading His people.

First of all, disturbance: "As an eagle stirreth up her nest." Then assurance that love will protect the disturbed ones as they falter: "fluttereth over her young". Then the call that those who are disturbed shall find their real purpose, that they might be taught to fly: "he spread abroad his wings" (RV). And finally that in all the process of adventure with the parent birds there is absolute safety: "He took them, he bare them on his pinions" (RV). The leading of the eagle – and here are the providential elements of God governing His people.

Let us retrace our steps and ponder in the light of the poetic revelation. Let us obey the suggestiveness of the illustration.

First of all, disturbance. I bring you to Deuteronomy 1:6. Moses says: "The LORD our God spake unto us in Horeb, saying, Ye have dwelt long enough in this mount." The mountain was Sinai. They had been there for over a year and were settling down to the privileges of the new covenant. It was the place of protection and blessing. They were content to stay and enjoy the peace and stability of the new life.

Then suddenly the command came to strike their tents and to be on the move: "Ye have dwelt long enough in this mount." The reason: they will never possess the land except they turn and face the wilderness. So Israel went towards the wilderness – that untrodden territory that always lies between the place of the vision and the good land.

When God speaks there is no room for dispute or deferment. The omnipotent Lord holds no conference – the providential care of Yahweh offers no explanation. "Get thee out of thy country, and from thy kindred, and from thy father's house, unto a land that I will shew thee." He does not ask if it is convenient. The call may come when circumstances are inauspicious – but come it does. We can be sure of one thing though – it does not come arbitrarily. God never disturbs merely for the sake of causing a disturbance . Every movement is with purpose. Every change is fraught with love. There would be no progress if there were no stirring up of the nest. God is more concerned for His people's progress than for their comfort.

Say what you will, this is God's method. He breaks in upon us in unexpected ways, perchance at unwelcome times, and leads us by unknown paths. So God broke in upon Abram in Ur, on Jacob in the house of Laban, on Moses in Horeb. As heaven willed, men who trusted God moved and wrought. In every true life there is the same witness. God leads His people like an eagle.

In the midst of the leading it may not be so evident and yet tomorrow brings the explanation of the past, and the next day we find the key to solve the mystery of today. Men without faith are blind to the unseen power that directs our lives – unbelief judges by fragments. Men of faith take the long view and see the providential care of God disturbing, provoking and bearing His people forward. Who is it that settles a man's habitation and calling? Why did we leave where we were? Who brought us to where we are?

There may be no light beyond the next step and yet there is assurance that the untrodden way will lead us to where we ought to be. Sinai may be good but Canaan is better. Our plans are broken down. Our highest motives have to be reconsidered. Our service is diverted and changed. Our very strength is turned to weakness, so that we may know the truth about our will and our wilfulness. The warmth and comfort of the nest is one thing, but God does not keep His people in cotton wool all the time. He takes away the props so that they may stand firm and have salt in themselves.

Come back to the figure. Watch the young eaglets as they struggle in the air, twisting and falling. Suddenly the peace and safety of the nest is gone and they are perplexed: "As an eagle stirreth up her nest." But mark the next step. It seems as though they will be lost, when suddenly the eagle swoops as swift as lightning and catches them on its broad wings. The children are borne back on the mother wings to the ledge and to the safety of the nest. It will happen again tomorrow and the next day, and as the process advances so the eaglets gain assurance. One day they will not struggle; one day they will spread their wings and mount up with the parent bird towards the sun. If the eaglet was left undisturbed in the security of the nest the latent powers which are divinely natural to the eagle would never be fulfilled – the law of the eagle would never be obeyed. So with advancing assurance the young become what their Creator intended they should be.

When a man comes to realise that in the disturbance of God there is progress, he will be assured. Bit by bit there is the certainty that by this method the powers of life are being developed. Step by step the process enables a man to discover how he may use the forces which are for him divinely natural – God bearing such an one on His pinions in the hour of weakness and perplexity. With humble but increasing confidence the soul is at rest and the spirit is at peace.

Piety on crutches is no good. Life in leading strings is not the same as following the leading of God. Circumstantial goodness is not the same as righteousness. In the end, religion is personal. One man's faith is not enough for two. Any man can be true whilst the sun shines and all is comfort and joy.

Of necessity our discipleship calls for independence, courage and sacrifice. We are not here to mould ourselves to this world but to master it. So the men of God must learn to face the tempest – prepared to be buffeted by storms, ready to mount upward and get above the forces which otherwise would bring them to doom.

As the eagle stirs up the nest and will not permit the young to fall into lethargy and sleep when they are full and satisfied, so the Lord disturbs His loved ones, contradicts their cherished plans, exposes them to forces which develop their character; puts strength into their spiritual powers, turns weakness into strength at last. As the eagle fulfils the law of the eagle which God has placed upon it, so His men fulfil the law of manhood, once perfectly revealed in the Man of Nazareth and now enjoined upon all those who have taken his name and seek to follow his discipline. Apart from him all life is exposed; apart from him it is hard and cold and dry. As Isaiah told it, he is the Refuge, the River and the Rock. God's eagle methods are exercised to make us like Him and to become to others what He is to us.

Of course men of unbelief have never been able to understand how God could so disturb those whom He is supposed to love. If God was really governing your life would He allow you to be so disturbed? or would He separate you from such a sacred relationship? or would He terminate such a successful venture?

But men of faith understand this. More than once they have read this: "... *strangers and pilgrims* on the earth" (Hebrews 11:13; 1 Peter 2:11). They know that those who follow the leading of the eagle are sojourners in tents ready to strike camp and move onward. And in the moving forward there is assurance – each experience brings a deeper conviction that somehow they are moving on the eagle wings of God; that somehow they are enwrapped by the great *motherhood* of God. Are you shocked because I said, "motherhood". Did you notice the change of pronoun in Deuteronomy? "As an eagle that stirreth up *her* nest, that fluttereth over *her* young ..." and then, "He spread abroad his wings, he took them, he bare them on his pinions" (RV).

Do you remember this in Isaiah 66:13? "As one whom his mother comforteth, so will I comfort you; and ye shall be comforted in Jerusalem." The motherhood of God, and the Fatherhood of God are merged in the leading of the eagle. And such as are God-governed in this way in their discipleship learn to venture with God in faith.

"Thy God bare thee, as a man doth bear his son ... who went before you in the way, to seek you out a place to pitch your tents in" (Deuteronomy 1:31-33, RV). If we have understood that rightly it means that the pitching of the tent at night is not accidental – that in some way God has been before us. In some sense He has inspected the terrain and has appointed the place of rest. According to Moses, God bears His people as a man does His son with infinite patience and tender compassion, accommodating His strength to their weakness, waiting for them in their slowness, halting with them in their perplexity.

Looking for the Lord

What is the effect of this God-governed life upon a man of faith – a man conscious of the leading of the eagle? Well, as it appears to me, he becomes a man who is undisturbed because he is always ready to be disturbed.

There is the counterpart of this in the New Testament. I bring you to the words of Jesus: "Let your loins be girded about, and your lights burning; and ye yourselves like unto men that *wait for their lord*, when he will return from the wedding; that when he cometh and knocketh, they may open unto him immediately" (Luke 12:35,36). *"Wait* for their lord ..." Hear the verse in the RV: "And be ye yourselves like unto men *looking for their lord* ..." To me that is better than waiting. Waiting seems to have about it a sense of quiescent inactivity, but about *looking* there is a sense of serene eagerness – a situation where there is no need if disturbance should come for a sudden and hasty scraping together a welcome for the returning Lord. Rather a serene and thankful opening of the door with a quality of immediateness because every day they were ready to be disturbed – every day they were ready for the knock, and every day the welcome was prepared and renewed.

It means that when life is lived on this level, where men are looking for their Lord in this spirit, then finality on any level is never reached. A man can never say, 'I am satisfied – life is realised'. A man can never say, 'I will now rest here under this juniper tree till I die'. The only hour of satisfaction and finality for such a man is the hour when the Lord is come and the man has looked into his Lord's face and has been changed into his likeness.

It means that all hopes and all intentions and all ambitions must be made subservient to the one great hope and the one great ambition. It means that every intention shall be unrealised, if the disturbance which halts the realisation is some new venture with the Lord or that glad hour when the Lord has come. It is a recognition that every other goal will be lost and cancelled for the sake of following the eagle and at last crossing into Canaan.

Therefore my brethren, ideally – and I am obliged to stress, *ideally*, it is a life in which all fear is checked, and every tremor is hushed to rest. In such a God-governed life, panic is outlawed. It illuminates every hour of sorrow, it soothes every agony, it lights with glory every dark cloud. In the day of frightfulness the heart is fixed. Fear may assault, but it cannot master. Sorrow may invade, but it cannot destroy. A man may rise in the morning and read his newspaper and know that the things which are temporal are being shaken. He will go out to his duty and is not afraid because he believes that somehow he is preceded by the God of the universe – in some mysterious way he is being borne upon the wings of the eagle. It is therefore a life dependent upon the unseen, a life that waits calmly for the disturbance of God. Loins girt, lamps burning, ready for the commanding word: "Ye have dwelt long enough in this mountain" – or the final shout and the trumpet of God.

This must affect a man's discipleship. It will result in a sincere separation to his Lord's will and a glad submission to His law. Will it not give immediateness, a thoroughness to every piece of work? God knows He may disturb me – intermediately or finally – and the thing He has commanded me to do may not be done. Therefore let me do it whilst the opportunity is here – redeeming the time – before it is gone and I be found to have neglected the one thing He has called me to fulfil, and His scrutiny shall bring me shame.

And it ought to make us patient. Patience in our souls, patience with our comrades, patience with God – not going before Him, but letting Him go before us. Patience does not say, 'Because he is coming I have no responsibility for the man next door or for the agony of the world in need of redemption.' Patience is haste upon the King's business led by the eagle, upward and sunward: restful haste, peaceful speed, graceful diligence. This is the ideal conception of the God-governed life. The writer is half ashamed to tell you that too often the ideal is lost and the goal is abandoned, and in the clear shining of the eagle way – it is left unfollowed.

One last word. It may be your experience to have heard the disturbing call of God. I do not know – it may be. Perhaps you tarried when you ought to have moved forward, consequently perhaps you have had a long weary wilderness instead. But now it could be that once again you are on the margin of the good land. May I urge upon you one thought from this meditation.

All your wilderness experience has been in the right hand of the Most High. All the disturbance has been under His government. Although you may not realise it, He is restoring the years which the 'cankerworm hath eaten'. "He careth for you." His covenant is "ordered in all things, and sure".

Faith will see the true focus: the intricacies of some present problem, the agony of some deep sorrow, the hush of some momentous decision to be taken. With all your bruises and wounds and disappointments, He will bear you on eagle wings until at last you can mount up sunward and be what God intended you to be. God grant that in your deepest heart you may feel it to be true.

Faith at rock bottom

AT the risk of wearying you, may I remind you of the principle upon which these studies are based. It is that in the book of Deuteronomy there are words which are central and fundamental to the discipleship of Christ. These words are spoken not incidentally and dispensationally but essentially and universally. They were true then and they are true now. In this chapter we are to think about faith – descending and then ascending.

There is no doubt that in the life of discipleship faith is the source of strength. Doubt cramps energy – trust is power. All things are possible to him that believes. Disciples are called to overcome the forces which apart from God would doom them.

When the saints are gathered for the final song of triumph on Mount Zion it is not going to a great bath chair rally! As their Lord is victorious, so are they to be. Remember the words of Jesus through his revelation to John:

"He that overcometh, I will give to him to sit down with me in my throne, as I also overcame, and sat down with my Father in his throne." (Revelation 3:21, RV)

Mark the quality of their victory: "As I also overcame." The Apostle John fixes the power which brings the victory:

"This is the victory that overcometh the world, even our faith." (1 John 5:4)

Faith is the assurance of things hoped for by the proving of things not seen. In order to have triumphing faith you must have the capacity to see the invisible. According to their vision, men are empowered.

Seeing the invisible

So it was with the heroes and heroines catalogued in Hebrews. Abraham left a certain city for a land he had never seen and did not know. He began the journey having no idea where it would lead. If there had been newspapers in the day of Abraham, one morning in the *Chaldean Times* an article would have begun like this:

> 'Our respected citizen Abraham is leaving us at the end of the week. When our correspondent asked him where he was going, he said he did not know. He has been counselled to seek medical advice.'

Measured by the wisdom of the hour the men and women of Ur would have said that Abraham was a foolish man – foolish to the point of instability. Yet Abraham was sure and calm. Why was he so sure of the unseen land? Because he was sure of the unseen God. When men see the invisible they do things which blind men would never contemplate.

Noah did a strange thing – he built a big liner in the middle of dry land. They never thought of building the "Queen Elizabeth" at Coventry – the harbour is a little shallow in dry weather! If there had been newspapers in the day of Noah, one morning in the *Mesopotamian Chronicle* there would have been a headline: 'Noah has gone mad!' When men see the invisible they do things which other men count strange, even contradictory – even lunatic. Noah was utterly sure of the unseen flood, because he was sure of the unseen God. Somehow he knew in his deepest heart that there is a madness which rightly named is the sublimest sanity.

Think of the man with the shepherd's crook who turned his back on all the splendour of Egypt, because he "had respect unto the recompence of the reward" (Hebrews 11:26). Somehow he was sure there is infinitely more value in the Messiah's reproach than in the honour of Pharaoh. "He endured, as seeing him who is invisible" (verse 27). He knew that sin has a short season – measured by the calendar of heaven.

Think of the man of Tarsus. He saw something which his companions could not – and he was never the same again. He tramped over rough roads, faced tempests, endured peril upon peril, more than once barely escaped with his life – because he was utterly sure of his King. "I know whom I have believed" (2 Timothy 1:12), he said.

"For I am persuaded, that neither death, nor life, nor angels, nor principalities, nor powers, nor things present, nor things to come, nor height, nor depth, nor any other creature, shall be able to separate us from the love of God, which is in Christ Jesus our Lord."   (Romans 8:38,39)

What a splendid confession of unshakable faith and what a life of enduring faithfulness came out of it.

But I think I know what you are thinking, for I am thinking the same myself. Not many of us live at that altitude – we rarely get above the snowline. Too often we are in the valley where the day is dull and the saffron scarce and the stream of life is sometimes rancid. Faith descends and we think thoughts and nurse doubts and do things which would make us ashamed in the presence of Abraham, Noah, Moses and Paul.

Why does faith descend? Why does it get dim? Why do disciples once strong, fail and falter? It is no new problem. Think of these two sentences: "Ye were running well; who did hinder you?" (Galatians 5:7, RV); "I have this against thee, that thou didst leave thy first love" (Revelation 2:4, RV). There are divers reasons – perhaps as many as there are different kinds of disciples. We cannot think of all, only some – and here are two.

The problem of fear

First of all, very often faith is assaulted by fear. Fear is insidious. It saps the strength, it weakens the nerve, it dilutes the resolution. Through fear men lose their grip and their optimism. High hopes are dashed and loyalty abandoned through fear.

Think of the people of God as they came to the margin of the good land. At Kadesh Barnea the spies went in to gain intelligence for the preparation of the campaign. They came

back with their reports. There were two – a majority report and
a minority report – almost identical. The majority report said,
'It is a good land, it flows with milk and honey, the grapes are
luscious, the rivers are beautiful; *but* there are walled cities and
giants in the land, we had better not go – let us make a captain
and go back to Egypt'. The minority report said, 'It is a good land,
it flows with milk and honey, the grapes are luscious, the rivers
are beautiful; it is true there are walled cities and giants, *but* we
are well able with God's help to take the land – let us go up and
possess it'.

The placing of the 'but' makes all the difference. It is to the
lasting shame of the people of Israel that they chose the majority
report – they were afraid of the forces which were in opposition;
their courage melted away. The Hebrew writer says that they
could not enter in because of unbelief. It tells us that eroded faith
is a barrier to possession.

And what made their failure so inexcusable was that they
had received so much evidence of the invisible God. Remember,
faith is the assurance of things hoped for by the proving of things
not seen. God had given them abundant proof of His power and
His compassion. He parted the Red Sea and destroyed their
enemies in it. He delivered them from Egypt with mighty power
– and yet here they are with no assurance about His ability to
deal with walled cities and giants. They dare not venture with
God. They forgot His providential care, but they remembered the
leeks and the onions and the garlic of Egypt. It is strange that
garlic has come to be the outward sign of some inward disgrace.
Let the gourmets beware!

Such was the tragedy of descending faith in the people of
God. They turned back from their high heritage through fear:
fear of the things which lie ahead; fear of losing the things which
lay behind.

Here is the issue. Dare we consult our own fears in the light
of this example of Israel? The local conditions have changed but
the principles remain. Why do men hold back from venturing in
faith with God? Sometimes it is through a fear that if they were

to act boldly with faith they might expose themselves to some deprivation – the loss of some material advantage. Or a fear that the difficulties might result in some hardship or opposition which they are not ready to endure. Or that if they declared themselves openly as faith demands then their reputation would be injured. Or the fact of acting in faith might mean the repudiation of some relationship or some indulgence which they fear to relinquish or which they long to keep.

But there are other fears. Fear of weakness – the continual failure to master forces which assault the spirit and crush the soul. Fear of the unknown – some physical disability, some bodily failure, some dark problem which no human agency is able to solve. Fear of the things which are coming upon the world – fear of violence, fear of evil, fear that perhaps after all, that which began best will end worse. Fears about the mystery of sorrow and pain – not only our own, but that of others. Fear of death – the last enemy; not the fear of death itself but fear of the scrutiny of life which death will bring at last before the judgement seat of Christ. Fears about some sudden upspringing of forces in a man's character, forces which are depraved and degenerate – slimy, devilish and hateful. All these fears have the effect of eroding faith and dimming the vision, so that failure hangs on the heart like an icicle and the soul is benumbed.

The problem of self-corruption

The other force which hurts and harms the faith of God's people is self-corruption. I bring you to Deuteronomy 4:

> "When thou shalt beget children, and children's children, and ye shall have remained long in the land, and shall corrupt yourselves, and make a graven image, or the likeness of any thing, and shall do evil in the sight of the LORD thy God, to provoke him to anger: I call heaven and earth to witness against you this day, that ye shall soon utterly perish from off the land whereunto ye go over Jordan to possess it; ye shall not prolong your days upon it, but shall utterly be destroyed. And the LORD shall scatter you among the nations, and ye

shall be left few in number among the heathen, whither the LORD shall lead you. And there ye shall serve gods, the work of men's hands, wood and stone, which neither see, nor hear, nor eat, nor smell."   (verses 25-28)

Notice the process: "When ... ye shall have remained long in the land ... [and have taken its blessings for granted] ... and shall corrupt yourselves ... and make a graven image ... and shall do evil in the sight of the LORD." Notice the whole sad process begins with self-corruption. What is self-corruption? It is giving or using the powers of your life for something which is lower than the highest and the best. It is the first step in backsliding.

When a man takes his eye from what he knows is the highest and is satisfied with something lower, be the distance ever so small, his faith is on the decline. It is not the situation of having the ideal and falling short of it. That is one thing, but it is not self-corruption. When a man corrupts himself he puts something lower as his idea of what God is and what God requires. When he is corrupted he thinks falsely of God and so the next step is upon him – he is making an image. He is making God after the pattern of his own ideal, and at last he does some evil thing which at the beginning he never intended to do.

It starts ever so slightly with the first cooling of the passion, the first diminution of our loyalty to Christ, the accepting of a compromise, the coming to terms with the sin which most easily besets us. This is the tragedy of a man who wears all the externals of discipleship but inwardly has lost the thrill, the passion and the devotion. He is content with the self-invented god because it is really a projection of himself into immensity – a magnification of his own thoughts and his own desires: a god made in man's image.

And what we ought to be concerned about is not the great gulf that exists between God and the man who does overt evil in the sight of the Lord, but we ought to be concerned about the first step on the descending path: the first dimming of bright faith – the first chill wind that blows through the ways of a man's life which once were warm with love. If that process goes on unhindered it results at last in that condition which the Hebrew writer calls being hardened by the deceitfulness of sin.

"If from thence ..."

If there were no more to say it would be a sad and a gloomy thing to ponder – but there is more to say. Come back to Deuteronomy 4:27,28 and the people of God mastered by insensate gods they made for themselves. Look at verse 29:

> "But if from thence thou shalt seek the LORD thy God, thou shalt find him, if thou seek him with all thy heart and with all thy soul."

"If from thence ..." Think where "thence" came to be for the people of God: some foreign land, far away from Zion – in the heart of idolatry, mastered by paganism, degenerating and descending. Men of vision – of the highest vision, men of noble passion and fair ideals; men languishing and lost. How can they sing songs of Zion in a strange land, scattered, forsaken and despised? But if from thence ...

You do not have to be a genius to see that this is the agony of broken discipleship in Deuteronomy. "Thence" is the word – it may be a long way back, where there seems to be no hope, where there seems to be no possibility of restoration, where the heart is chilled and the soul is fevered, where the poor wandering boy is eating swine's husks and his spirit is broken.

But Moses says there is no situation so hopeless, no condition so hard, no failure so dark – but if there is a search for God, He will be found, and being found, He will lift up and restore. "If from thence thou shalt seek the LORD thy God, thou shalt find him, if thou seek him with all thy heart."

There is in the New Testament a word which is the counterpart to "thence". It is in Hebrews 7:

> "Wherefore he is able also to save them to the uttermost that come unto God by him, seeing he ever liveth to make intercession for them."   (verse 25)

The word is "uttermost". "Uttermost" looks back to the deepest place of failure – it expresses the power to find the broken ones wherever they may be. "Uttermost" – it means that his priesthood descends deeper than the deepest sin, penetrates every barrier, removes every impediment, heals every wound and finds the forsaken and the weary – though they be fear-filled and sin-laden. It finds them and carries them through the tempest and over the rugged mountain to the place of succour and safety.

"How beautiful upon the mountains are the feet of him that bringeth good tidings, that publisheth peace; that bringeth good tidings of good, that publisheth salvation; that saith unto Zion, Thy God reigneth!"   (Isaiah 52:7)

Then because God reigns, the broken soul knows that he is not forsaken. It was "from thence" that the wandering boy came to himself and said: "I will arise and go to my father, and will say unto him, Father, I have sinned against heaven, and before thee" (Luke 15:18). Have you noticed he was never able to finish that sentence – the sentence was interrupted by the Father's embrace and the loving welcome. The plan to be a slave instead of a son was hushed and ended by the ministry of restoration. "If from thence ..."

Come back to those things we thought of at first – the fears which rack our souls and twist our hearts; the depths of life – suffering and weakness and failure; the sorrow and the perplexity – the frightfulness which fills us with heart failure; the mastering power of self and sin which cripple us and fill us with foreboding; the disappointments, the fellowship, once joy-filled, and now soured and saddened. What can we do as faith descends and the spirit sinks into depression?

The everlasting arms
I bring you to Deuteronomy 33:27 and the great song of Moses once again: "The eternal God is thy refuge, and underneath are the everlasting arms." It is that sentence to which we must now set our minds and hearts this day.

Let us enjoy a bit of exposition. In this sentence the word for "God" is the Hebrew *Elohim* – in this particular case standing for the unfathomable and immeasurable power of the Most

High, the intensive Hebrew plural word speaking of might and majesty. There is a difference between the words "eternal" and "everlasting" in this sentence. The word translated "eternal" here (*qedem*) has the meaning of being in the front – whether it be place or time. Inferentially it means the place of the sunrise, the place where the day starts – it is a word which, though it speaks of the forepart, looks back to the start. It would be true to the Hebrew, so I gather, if we translated it, 'The God of old is thy dwelling place', but it would be lacking the poetic sense of the word "eternal" and therefore the best way of expressing it is this: 'The God of the beginning is thy dwelling place'. The God of the morning – that morning when the stars sang together for joy in the mystery of creation.

It is saying then, that the God who was at the beginning and revealed Himself in power and glory and creative wonder – the God of way back, is nevertheless near and He is your dwelling place. The nearness of the great God is discovered and realised as the place where failing men may be at home. I use the word "home" deliberately because home is the place where you are *at home*. It is the place where all fear is banished, the place where there is security and rest, where there is peace and goodwill, where you move, not by the authority of dogmatism, but by the authority of love; where every door is opened for love's sake and where you can be true to yourself. At home there is no need for guile – for pretence – for window dressing. At home, as you are inwardly, so you are outwardly. If you think I have overstated it, may I give you another place where the word "dwell" is used and it has the meaning of 'being at home with':

> "The sinners in Zion are afraid; fearfulness hath surprised the hypocrites. Who among us shall dwell with the devouring fire? who among us shall dwell with everlasting burnings?"
>
> (Isaiah 33:14)

The question that Isaiah asks, "Who among us shall dwell with everlasting burnings?" means 'Who will be at home in the fire? Who will be able to survive and come out of it better and purer?' Not the sinners in Zion but such as have lived lives made incombustible by the quality of their living. Gold survives the fire, stubble is destroyed. One is at home with fire, the other is not. Dwelling means 'being at home with'.

The God of the morning is your dwelling place. The God of the beginning is with you now on the pathway. In spite of your recurring powerlessness, in spite of your faltering steps, in spite of your trembling heart – the God of beginning is your homestead. This is the God who said, "Let there be light", the God who divided the water from the water, the God who brought life and said, "Let us make man in our image". Light, water, life – it is the story of discipleship, the light of the truth, the water of baptism, the life of faith. This God is your dwelling place where broken men may be at home.

And then, "Underneath are the everlasting arms". The word "everlasting" (*olam*) seeks to describe the timelessness of God. Age-abiding, unchanged by the ages, passing through and beyond the ages and yet the same. Violating the calendars and the almanacs, it means, as well, the vanishing point – where the line passes out of sight: the concealed, that which lies beyond the uttermost effort to follow and understand – where thought and imagination are halted; something so broad and extensive as to be always outside of human experience and human endeavour – broader than the broadest reaching of human hands and hearts, deeper than the deepest descending of human frailty, everlasting: the strength unlimited, the enclosing power, the infinite tenderness of the God of the morning.

Now think of "underneath". This is the only place in the Bible where we find this word. The Hebrew term is found in other places and its meaning is not in doubt – it is very simple, it means 'bottom'. Associated with the meaning is the idea of going down, descending, falling, beating down, humbling, the depths, the deepest condition which your imagination or your experience can conceive; when you were right down, in sorrow, in anguish, in fear, in weakness, in suffering, in failure, the lowest level; when you said, 'I was never deeper down than now': listen – "underneath" – lower than that are the everlasting arms.

When faith was at rock bottom, the everlasting arms of God were underneath – underneath life with all its mystery, with all its seeming chancefulness, with its perplexity and contradiction. "Underneath are the everlasting arms." There is nothing outside the orbit of His will; there is nothing beyond the tenderness His care.

How can we say it? How can we tell it? Human syllables are not adequate. When we are falling fearfully and sadly, in the last reach of the descent when every support is giving way, when no finger is lifted to halt our falling, when no voice can stay our helplessness and when no glance of the eye can understand our agony; in the moment of our utter weakness, in the moment of final hopelessness – we fall – and we have fallen into the arms of God: cradled by the God of the morning, succoured at rock bottom.

And Moses goes on to proclaim that the God who is our refuge will bring to nought all the forces which are set upon hindering and harming us. He will thrust out the enemy. Fear like a black raven will drop dead, and old death riding on his pale horse is vanquished. So we may take the words of old – Moses' last words – and make them our own:

"Happy art thou, O Israel: who is like unto thee, O people saved by the LORD, the shield of thy help, and who is the sword of thy excellency! and thine enemies shall be found liars unto thee; and thou shalt tread upon their high places."

(Deuteronomy 33:29)

So here is the answer to our fears and foreboding. He is in the beginning – the beginning of this day and every day – until the cycle of running days is over and all the secrets of the ages are unveiled.

BOOK TWO
The pathway of prayer

1 |

Prayer – privilege and possibility
Luke 18:1-14

ONE word of explanation before we begin. In speaking about prayer I should not like you to think that I am posing as an expert on this subject. There are some things you can become expert about by careful and diligent study – by much reading, by continual discussion and comparison. Prophecy would be such a subject: by diligent study you become competent in the interpretation of prophecy.

But prayer is not like this. There is no way to learn to pray but by praying. We discover by use, we learn by practice.

I once knew an elderly man in Christ – I use the past tense because he has fallen asleep. He was poor judged by human standards and untutored; he had to be taught to read before he could ponder the word of God. I think he knew more about prayer than any man I have ever met. Poor and untutored, yes, but he was a mighty man in the ministry of prayer.

So, I have not written about prayer as an expert. I challenge no man's opinion, I question no man's method. I simply put it to you as it appears to me. So if perchance I should fall into dogmatic language it is not because I think this is the last word about prayer. All I say is, that which has helped me I hope may help you. There are problems about prayer and we hope that by sharing thoughts we may together find some consolation.

We begin dogmatically with a good sound Bible principle: "As [a man] thinketh in his heart, so is he" (Proverbs 23:7). It tells us that what a man thinks regulates what he does. A man's belief conditions his actions. My consciousness of anything controls my conduct towards it. My consciousness of a child conditions my conduct towards that child. My consciousness of a young woman conditions my conduct towards that young woman. If my consciousness is low my conduct will be low – and if my consciousness is high, resultantly my conduct will be higher.

In the city of Corinth in New Testament times there were sceptics. They did not believe in any other life than this life. They did not believe in any other world than this world and so they lived lives purely on the plane of the material – sensual and transient. They had a proverb: 'Let us eat, drink, and be merry, for tomorrow we die.' Their way of life arose directly out of their philosophy. "As [a man] thinketh in his heart, so is he." What you believe inevitably determines what you do.

This is true about prayer. What you think about prayer will decide whether you pray and how you pray and what happens as a result of your praying. So our business is first of all to consider what is the right teaching about prayer – its privilege and its possibility. This is the pathway we must tread if we are to come to a condition of prevailing prayer before God.

I do not know whether we want a definition of prayer, but when I was young they taught me that prayer was the raising of the heart and mind to God, and I have never felt the need to quarrel with that definition. In short, prayer is communication with God – a cry, uttered or unexpressed, which reaches heaven and the Majesty on High.

"No man hath seen God at any time …"

In Romans 1:20 the Apostle Paul says that men have evidence of the existence of God in the things which are created. There is evidence of power and intelligence in the things of nature – the divinity of God is marked on every tree and on every blade of grass. Nature proclaims the existence of eternal energy and transcendent wisdom. But I do not think you will be constrained to pray to eternal, limitless energy. Even when you see it marshalling stars and controlling seasons and presiding over the secret forces of the universe, I do not think you will pray to such a force in the way we think of praying. It is difficult to believe that a word of yours or mine could reach or affect such a stupendous intelligence. Standing by itself it becomes unthinkable. We may feel broken and bruised and need to pray, but somehow we cannot pray to the inscrutable force which is in nature. We know that Romans 1:20 is utterly true and the created things demand our wonder and our reverence – but it is not the whole story.

The whole story is that out of this stupendous intelligence has come a revelation which has changed the whole situation with a new dimension. This is it – and it is summarised for us in a verse in John's Gospel:

"No man hath seen God at any time; the only begotten Son, which is in the bosom of the Father, he hath declared him."

(1:18)

It means that out of the infinite spaces of eternity and from the mysterious and inscrutable intelligence of the invisible force has come a great love song. Behind the power and the precision of the great God of the universe there is abundant and abounding grace. Notice that phrase, "the bosom of the Father". It means the Father-heart of God, and out of that Father-heart of God the Son has spoken to men.

We know now, as with hushed spirits we ponder this Lord of revelation, that the one who has spoken out of the "bosom of the Father" is the one with wounded hands, and the mystery of pain upon his life, and the death of sacrifice enwrapping him like a garment – so that we may be able to come near to the great God of the universe and find pardon and peace and protection; so we may enter the presence of the great God and the place of prayer.

"Like as a father pitieth his children, so the LORD pitieth [has compassion on] them that fear him" (Psalm 103:13). We know that somehow in the fibre of our being we are undone. We are under the pollution and penalty of sin – lost and straying, broken and bereft.

And then we discover that underneath the eyes of fire there is the voice of love: "I am the good shepherd: the good shepherd giveth his life for the sheep." It tells us that the shepherd work of

God will never cease until the straying ones are brought home. There is pardon for sin and cleansing for pollution – there is power in place of paralysis.

So standing in the Son's revelation of the Father-heart of God, a man in his weakness and his utter need is constrained to draw near in reverent and filial fear to pray. It means we may come with all our bruises and our wounds and our impoverishment, and find grace to help in time of need. This is what I mean by privilege. The revelation creates the desire to pray. If you believe and if you feel this to be true it must affect your praying: "As [a man] thinketh in his heart, so is he."

To pray or to faint

But there is more to be said about the privilege of prayer. I bring you to Luke 18:1: "Men ought always to pray, and not to faint." On a point of exegesis, in the Revised Version instead of the word "*Men* ought always to pray", there is: "*They* ought always to pray." The change is important, for this reason. It reveals more clearly to whom the King was speaking. If you go back a few verses in Luke you will read this: "And he said unto his disciples ..." (17:22). Jesus then goes on to speak of the stress, strain and conflict of the life of discipleship.

You will see then that the word "Men" tends to detach his words from the immediate context whereas the word "they" includes it even more closely. They, the disciples, faced with the allied forces of opposition and ungodliness, "ought always to pray, and not to faint".

Notice what the King is doing. He is putting these two things in opposition. He declares that this is the alternative before a disciple – to *pray* or to *faint*. There are two groups only – there is no hint of a middle course. According to our understanding of the King's teaching, if men pray rightly they will not faint, and if they do faint, it will be because they have ceased to pray. So you can find your interpretation of prayer by the process of negation. Put simply, prayer is the opposite of fainting. Fainting is a sudden sense of weakness, helplessness; it is weariness – it is to feel the force of life ebbing away.

So by contrast you can define the effect of praying. It is to mount up with wings as eagles, to run and not be weary, to walk and not faint. Though the way be rough and rugged – perhaps walking amidst precipices – it is safety and assurance. This then is the King's great philosophy of life. There is no hour so dark, no temptation so subtle, no conflict so fierce – but that if I shall pray, then I shall overcome.

Now here is something to notice – that although praying is a privilege, right in the heart of the privilege there is necessity. "They *ought* to pray and not to faint." It is a privilege indeed, and yet it is a duty: *they ought*. It must mean that in God there is resource equal to every demand that can come upon those who trust Him. Men ought not to faint, because men ought to pray.

This then is the privilege of prayer. The inward impelling force is the realisation of our own need and the revelation of God's abundant solution, for love's sake. The Father-heart of God is making provision for every need of His children.

And then the necessity. If a man is suffering from a deadly disease and there is a certain remedy, but he refuses the remedy and dies, you could say he died of the disease. But it would be only half the truth. The real answer is that he died because he refused the remedy. This is our situation. Standing by ourselves we are bound to faint – to feel the vigour of life passing, beaten, broken down, disintegrating, descending and at last doomed. There is no middle course. "They ought always to pray, and not to faint." This is our privilege and our necessity.

If we understand it rightly and feel it to be true – it will control whether and how we pray.

"If ye abide in me ..."
Think next of *possibility* – that is to say, the purpose and the achievement of prayer. I will come to the point straight away and say that there are those who affirm sincerely that the sole purpose of prayer is subjective – that is, its object is to *change*

those who pray, to produce upon the character of those who pray something noble and uplifting, but nothing else. Now whilst I have the deepest respect for those who sincerely hold this view of prayer I am obliged to say that I think it to be utterly wrong, and in a sense a theory which is self-destructive.

When we were thinking about *privilege*, we brought to mind a simple but profound statement in John's Gospel. Let us do the same now while we are thinking about *possibility*. Here is a simple but profound statement of the King himself:

"Ask, and it shall be given you; seek, and ye shall find; knock, and it shall be opened unto you: for every one that asketh receiveth; and he that seeketh findeth; and to him that knocketh it shall be opened. Or what man is there of you, whom if his son ask bread, will he give him a stone? Or if he ask a fish, will he give him a serpent? If ye then, being evil, know how to give good gifts unto your children, how much more shall your Father which is in heaven give good things to them that ask him?"   (Matthew 7:7-11)

Now, if when I ask, I never have; when I seek, I cannot find; when I knock, no door is ever opened to me – then I am obliged to say with deep reverence that somehow I have been deceived. The words of the King are most explicit here. There is another quotation which is equally as remarkable:

"If ye abide in me, and my words abide in you, ye shall ask what ye will, and it shall be done unto you [caused to be]."
                    (John 15:7)

In that passage there is the condition, and then the achievement. The condition is this: "If ye abide in me, and my words abide in you ..." That demands a situation where the desires of the praying one harmonise with the purposes of God, and that harmony is brought about by living a practical life that is homed in God, and a spiritual life where the King may dwell and be at home. Where he may move by the authority of love, and where there is nothing to make his presence impossible, then given such a condition prayer becomes a method of co-operation with the great God of heaven. This, therefore, is the situation where God will answer the cry and the petition of the one who prays, understanding that He will not grant anything which hurts or harms those on whom His love is set. If in fact prayer has no objective value then these words only deceive me into thinking it has.

This alternative – that these are words of one who was sincere but deceived, is an alternative I cannot accept and nor can you. We do not believe he was deceived or a deceiver. The Bible says that heaven and earth may pass away but his word cannot. It appears to me that if you deny the possibility of objective prayer you have denied the word of the King.

But think about it along the line of reason. I am the first to recognise the subjective value of prayer. I know well enough that praying does affect the inward condition of those who pray. It does change us as we practise prayer – of course it does. Those who speak with God cannot escape bearing the mark of it, like Moses in the mount.

But here is the argument – that the subjective value and effect of prayer arises out of a conviction that when men speak to God He hears and answers their prayer. If a man prays for something it is because he has faith in the God to whom he prays.

It seems to me that the subjective value of prayer arises out of its objective value, and if you can demonstrate its subjective value, it follows therefore that you have presumptive evidence that prayer has an objective purpose.

Again most people who pray objectively – that is believing that God grants their petitions and that external things are changed by prayer – I say people who pray like that are affected in themselves: they are changed, often they are uplifted and ennobled. Now if there is no such possibility that God answers in that way, then it means that belief in that which is untrue is able to produce a character which is true and noble. Such a proposition is untenable.

And then there is another fact which cannot be denied. It often happens that people who believe only in the subjective value of prayer and deny its objective value, at last give up praying altogether. I know of three examples of this myself. It seems that no man continues to ask if at last he is convinced that the only effect is an effect upon himself. That is what I meant when I said that the theory was at last self-destructive.

Then go back to Luke 18 and think of the unjust judge in the parable. The parable is an exposition of the meaning of prayer by the use of contrast – contrast all the way through. All that the unjust judge was, God is not. The judge was unjust, careless and indifferent – concerned only with his own peace and security. By contrast God is revealed as being susceptible, righteous and just – and mark the word of Jesus, "longsuffering over them". He will "avenge" – and the word does not mean take revenge, but do justice to – and the King adds the word "*speedily*". It reveals that God is one who answers the heart uplifted in prayer and Godward, not reluctantly, but He is ready to hear and answer the weakest, feeblest, faintest cry.

So we form our understanding of the possibility of prayer – first by our doctrine of the nature of God, as we thought about it under privilege, then by the gracious words of the King himself – tenderly spoken and substantiated by his own life, death and resurrection. Then finally, we are reassured by the history and experience of men and women of God who have asked and received, sought and found, and have knocked and had the door opened. Today science makes experience the universal test of truth and reality – and if that be true we are more than right to include in our testimony the experience of the people of God who prayed and were answered.

The history and experience of God's servants

Think of some examples in the Bible: think first of all of Hannah, wife of Elkanah (1 Samuel 1). Hannah was a woman with a broken heart. She was the first wife, but her husband took a second. It was legal but not wise. There are some female temperaments that might be able to agree in such circumstances, but in this case it was not so. Peninnah, the second wife, was a woman with a bitter tongue and poor Hannah was a woman who was barren, and the target for Peninnah's jealousy. So in the words of the narrative, she "provoked her sore, for to make her fret".

She knew what she needed – she needed a man-child. It was no good explaining to Hannah that the laws of nature cannot be changed or that the laws of chance cannot be manipulated. Somehow she had the idea that the power which shuts the womb can open it. The power which makes barren can make fruitful. She in bitterness of soul, prayed to the Lord and wept sore. When she went back from Shiloh her countenance was sad no more – she had cast her burden on the Lord. It was not in vain, and Hannah never ceased to give thanks, in the person of Samuel her child serving God.

Think of King Asa (2 Chronicles 14:8-15). You will recall his story. Suddenly he found himself in great trouble. He was a good king and everything was going well when out of the blue the Ethiopians came against him with a great army. Humanly speaking defeat was certain. Asa was helpless but not hopeless. He knew that the poverty of *our* resources is no problem to God. Asa sought a link with God.

His prayer is one of the most daring in the whole of the Bible. He said:

> "LORD, it is nothing with thee to help, whether with many, or with them that have no power: help us, O LORD our God; for we rest on thee, and in thy name we go against this multitude. O LORD, thou art our God; let not man prevail against thee."
>
> (verse 11)

What he meant was, 'We are inadequate, but we have come. We are weak, but we are at your disposal. Our failure will be your failure'. It was a bold plea, but it was answered with a great victory over Zerah and the Ethiopian hosts. The battle was not Asa's but God's and so was the triumph – but it needed Asa's faith.

Think of Joshua. He was a great soldier and a great servant of God. Under his command Israel had victories at Rephidim and Jericho. When they came to Ai it seemed like child's play by comparison. The intelligence corps said it was not a serious business at all, only a few men would be needed – there was no need to trouble the Almighty.

You know the story. They went out as though they were going to a Sunday School outing, and came back helter-skelter, licking their wounds. Joshua was dumbfounded but he took his defeat to God. You will want to remind me that Achan's sin was at the bottom of the trouble, but perhaps the root of the failure was the lack of prayer. If Joshua had taken the matter to God first, he would have discovered the hidden danger before the battle, instead of after it. They discovered their need too late. There is something about success that makes men self-confident, and self-confidence is fatal to discovering your need.

I bring you to the New Testament and Acts 9. The Lord is speaking to Ananias:

"Arise, and go into the street which is called Straight, and enquire in the house of Judas for one called Saul, of Tarsus: for, behold, he prayeth." (verse 11)

Although I have no doubt that Saul had prayed all his life, it is as though God meant: 'Mark this wonder, Saul of Tarsus is praying; he is being converted – he has discovered his need.' God told Ananias that this sign of praying was proof that the arch-persecutor had become a true disciple. Doubtless he had prayed before as a proud Pharisee, but now for the first time as a broken, repentant sinner. "Behold, he prayeth ..." With God this was conclusive.

Now I confess that from these examples it is possible to draw a wrong conclusion. It might be concluded that the only time we ought to pray is when we are in dead trouble. Such a view would be dislocated and unbalanced. The right conclusion is to see that men begin to pray rightly when they have discovered their dependence on God.

A man is usually more honest with himself in the day of need than in the day of satisfaction. A real sense of need has a way of laying bare the hidden workings of the soul. Defences are broken down, the masks are off and the artifices with which we cloak our motives are torn away. We do not have to be in dead trouble before we can discover our dependence on God.

Elijah needed God desperately on Mount Carmel but he knew his dependence on God before that. Men like Elijah may appear suddenly but they are not made in a day. The open victory is the fruit of secret prayers and born out of the knowledge of deep need.

Think of Daniel. Three times a day he prayed to God at the open window (Daniel 6:10). He did this when all was well with him, perhaps because he knew that the crisis would come, which when it came, would discover the hidden flaws and lay bare the source of his strength. The crisis sometimes tries all things. In one day a man may reap the harvest of a lifetime. The faith of Daniel was not a flash in the pan. His reliance on God was not born suddenly. Usually people who pray effectively in a storm have discovered the need in fine weather. Desperation is better than despair, but the best course is to have commerce with heaven before the storm envelops us. It is good to pray when we are in the darkness but it is better to walk in the light. Very often open victory is the fruit of secret prayer over a long time. Daniel's secret was the ministry of the open window: when the crisis came Daniel had nothing to alter; there was no panic. He continued to do then what he had always done. He went to the open window and he gave thanks, it says, "as aforetime" (verse 10). He did not suddenly need to change his life.

Of course that would not be true of everybody. I can think of a man, I won't tell you his name, but I reckon if the crisis like that had come to him, he would have shut the window, drawn the blinds, bolted the door and made his will. Daniel was ready for that day of crisis because he was ready every day. He stole an advance march against the enemy by discovering his need early when he faced the king's wine (Daniel 1). He knew what to do when he faced the king's wine, so God delivered him when he had to face the king's lions. That was the experience of Daniel: a praying man at the open window.

The need for conviction

Now I mention all these examples because I wanted to say this to you in conclusion. There are some people who will tell us that these persons and many others like them were all no doubt sincere, but somehow they were mistaken. Now if that be true – that the testimony of saints and seers, of prophets and priests, of psalmists and martyrs – if all this is to count for nothing, then we ought to say: 'May God help us to share their delusion (if they were deluded), because their delusion has been the cause of some of the noblest characters, and the most effective dynamic and some of the best work that has ever been done on the face of the earth in the name of God.'

But you do not believe that, and nor do I. These people were not mistaken. Let nobody rob you of your conviction that these great things which they did were done because of the power of prevailing prayer. And let us remember again that the conviction that this is true is based firmly on the doctrine first of all of the nature of the Fatherhood of God.

Let us go back over our reasons in this matter of *privilege* and *possibility*. Our conviction about prayer is based first of all on the realisation of the nature of the Fatherhood of God; then on the declaration of Jesus Christ, the King himself; then on the history of the experience of the saints.

As you think in your heart about prayer – so will you pray. And as you are conscious of its *privilege* and *possibility*, so you will be able to come next to its *preparation* and *practice*.

2 |

Prayer – the preparation and practice
Matthew 6:1-15,31

W
HEN I say 'preparation', let me explain what I do *not* mean. Suppose I am to preside at the breaking of bread service one Sunday and on the Saturday afternoon a brother rings me up and says, 'Brother Gillett, if you were thinking of calling upon me to pray tomorrow morning, I should be glad if you can let me know now so that I can prepare what I am going to say'. He means, 'Let me compose my sentences and let me polish my phrases'. Now I am not complaining one bit about such preparation. It is better to prepare and speak a well thought out prayer which meets the need, rather than to neglect it and then fumble and fail in consequence. It is true sometimes that this kind of preparation produces a prayer which is rather decorous and formal, but not always by any means – it is proper and right where it is necessary.

The only reason I bring it up is to remark that when I say 'preparation', I do not mean this kind of preparation. I do not mean getting ready to pray on some special occasion. I mean the preparation which touches our life and so makes us ready to pray at all times.

Let me put it to you in another way. There are certain great facts in life which make it possible for us to come to God in prayer and it is our response in daily life to those facts which prepares us to pray.

Before we proceed to examine this point, may I ask you to recall another great Bible principle – it is this. In the final analysis the truth about God and His purpose is not truth in the abstract. That is to say, it is not revealed to us just to inform us; it is not revealed just for us to learn; it is not revealed just so that we can speculate and discuss. Truth always sets up a claim upon us. By its very nature it makes a demand. Sometimes we speak of obeying the truth. It is not just something to be stored and labelled. The real purpose of spiritual truth is to change us and make us like God. The object of truth is godliness – Godlikeness.

Truth's claim upon us
The truth we learn should become incarnate in our lives. A man who speculates but never does, is half false already. The proportion by which a life is changed and sanctified by the truth is the proportion to which the individual is prepared for praying. Let us look at it more closely.

Think of some of the great facts of the truth: the Fatherhood of God, the mediation of the Son as Saviour and High Priest, the activity of the Holy Spirit in the word of God which is the light of our life. How we respond to these things will regulate our preparation for prayer. The measure of our response will be the measure of our preparedness.

Think again. God is our Father. How do we respond to that? The essential feature of a father-child relationship is that the child is the extension of the father. Fatherhood is life given; Sonship is life received. In the ideal relationship, sons ought to be like their father. So we call ourselves the children of God, and yet sometimes we are very far from being like Him: you would be hard put to see the identity.

Again Jesus said once: "Fear not little flock; for it is your Father's good pleasure to give you the kingdom." In that short sentence God is revealed as Father, Shepherd and King, and when men once saw it superlatively in Jesus, the old things burst forth with a new beauty such as humanity had never dreamed of. I say that, so when we seek to answer the claim of that revelation, we are being prepared for prayer.

Let me illustrate. How can we pray, *"Thy kingdom come"* if in some way we are rebelling against the King? How can we pray for the coming of the kingdom and at the same time hinder the development of the kingdom values in our own life – even love, joy and peace. How can we pray for the King's victory if we are nursing in our life one of the things against which the King is fighting?

Think of the Shepherd. It is the sheep's part to be content with the pasture which the Shepherd appoints. If I am not content and insist on regarding everything as drudgery, then I am ill prepared to pray. If I am content to go where the Shepherd leads, whether it be through the desert or by the still waters, content because he leads, then I am being prepared to pray.

Think of the mediation of the Son. In 1 Corinthians 1:30 the Apostle Paul has written:

> "But of him are ye in Christ Jesus, who of God is made unto us wisdom, and righteousness, and sanctification, and redemption."

How do I answer the claim of that great truth? Righteousness is rightness of conduct which arises out of sanctification which is rightness of character. Paul is saying that the King is the source of that righteousness and that sanctification. He once said: "Christ liveth in me." He meant that the life of Christ was to be reproduced in his own life. Now when the indwelling Christ calls us to some new duty, some new responsibility, some new enterprise, how do we respond? If we respond with a ready consent, then we are being prepared to pray. But if we refuse, prayer then becomes most difficult.

What makes us refuse? Some thing which we ought to repudiate but never do? Some relationship which pleases us but which is spiritually dangerous? Some indulgence which we cannot master and might master us? Some procrastination which robs us of our resolution? How difficult it is to pray when forces such as these dominate us.

Think of the Holy Spirit's revelation of God's purpose in this holy word. Part of the true preparation for prayer is a sincere response to the fact that the Son of God will soon burst upon the world with flaming advent glory. We often say we long for his coming. But dare we examine our deepest thought upon that affirmation? Would we be very upset if he postponed his coming for say another twenty years? There are so many *things* to do and life is so full of interest, and we have just fallen in love or we have just been married, or graduated, or fixed on the date of retirement. I know the problems and the feelings. You are right to fall in love and you are right to be married or to graduate or to retire and may God bless you, but you ought always to recognise that all your activities may be interrupted at any moment by the appearance of the King. The present joy will be superseded by the greater joy. The present ambition must be subservient to the greater ambition. The man or woman who truly looks for and longs for the coming of the King, is best prepared for prayer, because in order to pray prevailingly I must live in the hope of that day when all the present pain and sorrow will be ended.

If you have true compassion for humanity, if you can bring your sensitivity into touch with the world's agony, if there is in your heart a hot turbulent protest against the wickedness of evil men, then you will be driven to prayer for the people in your street and for the world, that the glory and judgement of God may come and His government be triumphant in the earth. When the Spirit-revealed word creates in your heart such an agony and such a desire, do not check it, for that is to grieve the Spirit indeed. As the glory of the kingdom flames and flashes before us in the word of God, and as the demon of fear comes gibbering at the windows of the world, and as faith grows dim and love waxes cold – those who "love his appearing" are driven to pray for his coming. But we cannot truly pray for his coming in the world, unless we are willing to have him established in our hearts. One is a preparation for the other.

So then I emphasise that as it appears to me, preparation for prayer in the real sense is no slight, spasmodic, superficial thing. It is the supreme part of life. It is certainly not that we have to be perfect before we can pray, but there are hindrances to prayer which need to be removed in order for prevailing prayer to be achieved. To put it to you bluntly – to be wilfully unsubmitted is to be painfully unprepared. To flirt with wrong things is to make praying very difficult. To nurse an unconfessed sin is to create an ice barrier on the pathway of prayer.

If you have ever been in that position then your experience will have taught you how impossible it is to draw near in prayer. We know we ought to but somehow we cannot. We intend to clear the obstacle and fall down in pleading but we keep procrastinating. We try to forget, but somehow the controversy will not go away.

David understood it and told it in Psalm 32: "When I kept silence, my bones waxed old through my roaring all the day long. For day and night thy hand was heavy upon me: my moisture is turned into the drought of summer" (verses 3,4). The controversy was sustained; it could not be hidden. As you know, in the end David acknowledge his failure and the breach was healed and the pathway was cleared. The window was opened and commerce with heaven was restored. So at last he says in verse 6: "For this shall every one that is godly pray unto thee in a time when thou mayest be found."

No – I am not saying that you can pray only when you are free from guilt, but I am saying that when we practise guile that is a tremendous handicap in the path of prayer. David says: "Blessed is the man ... in whose spirit there is no guile" (verse 2). So clean hands and a pure heart are best for those who seek to be alone with the great God. Hearts can be lifted to the Majesty on High, without being afraid, reverently indeed, but without dread.

Practical issues
Come now to *practice*, and I want this to be genuinely practical. I bring you to Matthew 6:

"And when thou prayest, thou shalt not be as the hypocrites are: for they love to pray standing in the synagogues and in the corners of the streets, that they may be seen of men. Verily I say unto you, They have their reward. But thou, when thou prayest, enter into thy closet, and when thou hast shut thy door, pray to thy Father which is in secret; and thy Father which seeth in secret shall reward thee openly. But when ye pray, use not vain repetitions, as the heathen do: for they think that they shall be heard for their much speaking. Be not ye therefore like unto them: for your Father knoweth what things ye have need of, before ye ask him." (verses 5-8) Now we must not think our Lord was teaching that there is something essentially wrong in praying in a synagogue or at the corner of the street. No, what he is warning against is that kind of praying which obtrudes itself upon other men's notice – praying that desires to be observed. Notice his gentle satire: "They have their reward." What he meant was, 'They pray in order to be seen of men and they have been seen of men'. What they wanted, they received. They have been paid in full.

The important teaching is the instruction to which this warning is a background: "When thou prayest, enter into thy closet, and when thou hast shut thy door, pray to thy Father which is in secret." Evidently the King is teaching that for his disciples there should be, if possible, a place of prayer and a method of prayer, so that every third party is excluded and the disciple may pray alone with God through the High Priest.

It is, of course, possible to pray anywhere at any time under any conditions. I know a man in Christ in a very busy job and he told me that he has breaks of say thirty seconds between one action and the next, and in those thirty seconds he utters a short prayer: thirty seconds of sanctuary in which he finds God. But in this passage our Lord is teaching us about the need for an inner chamber and a closed door. Prayers in secret tend to be more real than prayers in public and generally more free from drowsiness. So the instruction seems to be stressing the need for a process which ensures separation, seclusion and secrecy. In other words the formation of a habit of prayer.

It is sometimes said that habits are in themselves less valuable because they are habits, but the truth is, it does depend upon what the habit is about. After all, a habit is only something you do habitually, and to pray habitually is just what the King enjoins upon his disciples: "They ought always to pray, and not to faint"! The Apostle Paul says: "Pray without ceasing." This is not occasional, spasmodic, irregular prayer – it is habitual.

It is not possible to make inflexible rules about the place, the time and the method. Individual circumstances will decide these issues. But they must be decided with honesty and integrity. If somebody can honestly spend only three minutes at the beginning of the day with God, then if that three minutes is sincere and true, God can do a lot in a short time. But the person who gives three minutes only when they could well give fifteen in prayer and meditation, is not very likely to move many mountains.

Again the place does not matter so long as it provides some kind of solitude where the faculties of mind and heart are unfettered – and it follows, therefore, that if possible the place should be familiar and the same every day, so that it will not offer any distraction. The place we know well will not cause our mind to wander to outside things.

The method must suit our needs. We should cultivate the method which helps us most to pray rightly. Some people may prefer to speak aloud, while others would commune only through the mind. The attitude or posture is again a matter for individual judgement, remembering that we should choose the position which enables us to concentrate most easily. If you suffer from rheumatism, then kneeling is a bad position, for it will focus your mind on the pain in your knees instead of on God your Father. It is not a sin to be comfortable whilst at prayer, rather it is sensible.

I find in my own case that it is most suitable for me to sit. If there is no room where you may go for solitude and silence – and I know how that sometimes it is a real difficulty – if there is no place in the open where you may go and be alone with God, then the only thing to do is to try to cultivate the capacity to provide an open space where you can withdraw even in the presence of others. This is not easy and for those who are not experienced in the habit of prayer, the real inner chamber is a great boon.

Praying is an exercise which demands that every faculty shall be at its best and therefore if you can do it, it is good to pray when you are most alert and most alive. Right at the end of the day when the eyes droop and the mind is full of slumber is not best for concentrated prayer. Two minutes of lay-me-down-to-sleep prayer is alright – but it should not be the main prayer of the day, though in a busy life it sometimes is. The trouble is that drowsy prayer is not the prayer which is disciplined, concentrated and earnest. I must remind you of some words written about the King: "And in the morning, a great while before day, he rose up and went out and departed into a desert place, and there prayed." It shows us that prayer is a serious thing involving deliberate and conscious dedication. It is not a by-product of life; it is at the centre of life.

What shall we pray about?
It seems to me that we may pray about anything which is upon our heart and hopefully within the sphere of God's will. I mean, if we know for sure that there is something which is against God's will, we ought not to pray about it.

In the world men tend to divide their lives into that which is spiritual and that which is secular. In the life of the disciple that kind of a division is not justifiable. No part of our lives is shut out when we are shut in with God.

Because He is our Father, we pray as children and there is an artlessness about children's prayers which it is helpful to mark. I think it is true that as our life becomes more responsive to the great facts that make praying possible, so our petitions will probably get fewer. We may cease to pray about some things which at one time in our lives seemed to be so important. It may well be that with experience the approach about praying for our needs may change also. Experience may change our attitudes.

Again, let me illustrate with a homely example. In a certain ecclesia there was a sister who always used to pray for a fine day for the Sunday School outing. Of course, sometimes it was fine and sometimes it rained cats and dogs! One day when arrangements were being made for the outing, the Superintendent said to the elderly sister, 'And sister, have you prayed for a fine day?' And she replied: 'No – I have stopped asking God to make our day fine, for I have realised it may be His will to make it wet for other people's sake. What I have prayed is that in making our choice of the date, you will have enough sense to choose one of the days that God has decided to make fine!' It may make us laugh, but notice the change in approach. It may be on a low level but it illustrates the point. Prayer has its place in the infinitesimals of life.

Nehemiah prayed about building a wall. He prayed about his work. There are those who reserve prayer for desperate occasions, but it is not the best kind of prayer. In prayer, a man may go over his life and lay it all before God – small and great. Prayer sanctifies commonplace things and ennobles menial tasks, so that you do not mind that they seem so commonplace and menial. Pray about anything and experience will tell you before long what you can leave out of your prayers. Mere whims and foolish desires will appear in their true light and will be dropped in prayer. It is no use praying to go in one direction and then set your feet in the opposite direction. Nehemiah prayed about his work and then used all his wits and his skill to make it happen. It is no good praying about your work and then neglecting it.

Prayer has the effect of increasing vision and developing judgement. You will come to know what to pray about, but in the word of God there are clear guidances about what we ought to include in our praying. We ought to pray for our brethren and sisters. Jesus did, and so did Paul. We ought to pray for the word of God that it "may run and be glorified". We ought to pray for the ecclesia of Christ and those who have responsibility therein. Very often, praying is better than criticising.

We ought to pray for the coming of the kingdom of God. We ought to pray for those who have been set in authority over us in the civil government. We ought to pray for the sick and the isolated. There are those who, so to speak, have a natural right to our prayers – those in our own family whom we love and for whom we may be responsible. Job prayed for his children lest they perchance in their living did some wrong thing. Praying for all kinds of things calls for sympathy, understanding and watchfulness, being keen-eyed in seeing the needs and trials of others and remembering them before God in the secret place.

I know some brethren and sisters who keep a list of things they want to pray about. They do not feel it is right to throw one great careless bundle before God in prayer, but each need is singled out – each person individually remembered before the throne of grace. I have a prayer list of people for whom I pray every day. I find it is much better than leaving it to chance.

Paul says: "God shall supply all your need (*every need of yours*, RV) according to his riches in glory by Christ Jesus" (Philippians 4:19). "Every need" seems to suggest all kinds of things. May I say now that of course praying involves other things besides petitions: worship, thanksgiving, communion; but in this section we are thinking mostly about petitions – about asking for blessings and helps of various kinds.

Preconditions for prayer

There are two preconditions for prayer of which I am thinking just now. One is in Matthew 5:

> "Therefore if thou bring thy gift to the altar, and there rememberest that thy brother hath ought against thee; leave there thy gift before the altar, and go thy way; first be reconciled to thy brother, and then come and offer thy gift."
>
> (verses 23,24)

It seems clear that no gift and no prayer can be received by God if the offerer has a heart which is hardened against another of God's children. An unforgiving spirit makes prayer void. Reconciliation clears the pathway. The refusal to be reconciled bolts the door. The same principle is revealed in Psalm 66:18: "If I regard iniquity in my heart, the Lord will not hear me" – meaning that if I cling to sin it is no good coming in the guise of righteousness. In a way the judgement seat of God is sometimes in the secret place. What I mean is this. Sometimes forgotten and unforgiven sins start into life when we begin to pray. Praying needs a conscience which is set on dwelling in the light. Or put another way – he who comes to God for mercy must himself be merciful. The petitioner for grace must be gracious.

The other condition is the need to pray in faith. Atheists cannot pray; agnostics find it hard. The King once said: "All things are possible to him that believeth." Faith is trust. It is not a speculation, an option, a pious guess. Jesus said: "Therefore I say unto you, What things soever ye desire, when ye pray, believe that ye receive them, and ye shall have them" (Mark 11:24).

In the letter of James, doubt is double-minded and unstable. It is like a troubled sea – storm tossed and driven by the wind. Such a man gets nothing from his prayers because he is double-minded and doubting.

Then we must learn this – *it is possible to ask amiss.* "Ye ask, and receive not, because ye ask amiss, that ye may spend it in your pleasures" (James 4:3, RV). Evidently God takes notice not only of what we ask for but also why we want it. God looks at the heart and we have to face it, there are some hearts that will have difficulty in finding an audience with Him. The unbelieving heart has no access. The unforgiving heart is shut out. The self-seeking heart is halted. So the message is: ask believingly in accordance with the law of faith. And do not be afraid of asking. The King said, "Ask, and ye shall receive". Paul said: "In nothing be anxious, but in *everything* by prayer and supplication with thanksgiving, let your requests be made known unto God."

As I have said already, prayer is not all asking – it is thanksgiving and worship and contrition and submission – but it certainly includes asking. It is sometimes said, 'Why do we need to ask if God knows what we want before we ask Him?' Why pray if He knows? Because asking is different from giving information. It is one thing to inform; it is another thing to beseech in faith. It is revealed to us that although the God of heaven knows our needs before we ask Him, notwithstanding He waits to be asked before He distributes the gifts that supply our every need.

"Your Father knoweth what things ye have need of, before ye ask him. After this manner therefore pray ye ... give us this day our daily bread."   (Matthew 6:8-11)

Jesus is saying that because God knows our needs before we ask Him and is willing to answer them, the more we ought to ask Him. So when you pray have faith in God – it is something He never dishonours.

In Leviticus chapter 10 you can read of two men who offered strange fire before the Lord and were destroyed. We must always regard prayer seriously. Try to avoid the mechanical and the perfunctory. The Bible says God responds to prayers which are fervent: "The effectual fervent prayer of a righteous man availeth much." Intensity is part of the law of prayer. You remember, God hates the lukewarm. It is easy to shine, it is more difficult to burn. God is found most by those who seek Him with all their heart. He is not found by those who are flippant, merely curious, self-reliant and intellectually proud.

Speak to God in simplicity. Leave the eloquence to the place of public prayer. God does not want a lecture, He wants a prayer. We do not have to persuade God, but He likes us to ask faithfully and fervently.

The pattern prayer: peace, purity and power

THERE will be no dispute that the prayer which begins "Our Father, which art in heaven ..." is the pattern prayer. It was uttered by the King in response to the question from his next of kin – his apostles – "Lord, teach us to pray". So he said: "When ye pray, say ..." I am not sure why we never or hardly ever offer this prayer as it stands. At least we never seem to do it in our meetings. I do not think it is a calculated policy to avoid it, but more a matter of practice by default. Some people tell me that we do not use it because the churches use it. That makes me sad that we should allow the practice of an apostate church to determine what we do – but never mind, let us leave it there.

It seems that the Lord gathered together in this prayer the things which his disciples knew best about God – the things which are central in their relationship with Him. He has placed these central things in such relationship to each other so as to reveal the whole plane of prayer: that is how we ought to pray, and that is why it is a pattern prayer. When you have prayed it intelligently, searchingly and sincerely, you have prayed for everything and about everything. Each petition can be taken separately and developed; and it is inclusive and fulfils in itself a great ideal of God's purpose. All the vital petitions which may be scattered through the human mind and embedded in the human heart, provoked by faith, are gathered here and woven into one whole. The indexes are wonderful and revealing. Elaborated they become an inspiration; conjoined they become a masterpiece.

So let us ponder now the structure of the prayer: "Our Father which art in heaven" (Matthew 6:9). The thing to stress right at the beginning is that this invocation applies to, and is connected with, all the petitions in the prayer: not just the things which have to do with God Himself but just as much those things which have to do with human need – just as much with the provision, pardon and protection of the second half as with the worship and praise of the first half.

The next thing to remark on in general is that the qualifying phrase, "as in heaven, so on earth" (Matthew 6:10, RV) applies not only to the kingdom to come but to all the petitions which have preceded it. So it means: 'Thy name is hallowed – as in heaven, so on earth'; 'Thy kingdom come – as in heaven, so on earth'; 'Thy will be done – as in heaven, so on earth'. These three petitions, in a way, describe a process of development in the life of the one who prays, before being gloriously realised in the development of God's purpose on earth when His government is established with the coming of the King. As God's name is hallowed and reverenced in the life of the disciple, so God's kingdom becomes the master passion of his life – and so as the kingdom values are realised and incarnated, God's will is done. There is a sense also in which all the human need described in the second half is included in the first, though it is not expressed there. The point is that as and when God's victory is accomplished in the world, all the needs of men will be met and fulfilled.

We must now be more particular about the first three petitions.

"Our Father"

The Fatherhood of God is not a verbal device, a figure of speech, an accommodation. "Like as a father pitieth his children, so the LORD pitieth them that fear him." This tells us that God is like a father – but being like a father is not fatherhood. Analogy is not identity. Fatherhood means begetting a child. Many a man has behaved like a father to another man's child but that does not make him a father. Fatherhood is life given; sonship is life received. Having fatherly feelings is not enough. It means that once in the long process of the centuries God begat a child. That holy thing was in the very truest sense the Son of the Highest. The reality of God's Fatherhood is not diminished when it is applied to His other children.

The children of God are a real family, based not on the tie of some artificial combination, but based upon ties of divinely natural affinity. That is to say, it is a real family and God is a real Father. You will perhaps have heard of the Associated Society of Locomotive Engineers and Firemen, or the Weavers and Woolpackers Association. They are trade unions in Britain and these trade union members sometimes call themselves brethren, but it is an artificial combination.

The family of God is not like that. Jesus once turned to a little group of disciples – ordinary people they were, men of like passions with ourselves; failing men, even sometimes blundering men, but men who loved him truly, and to those he said: "Whosoever shall do the will of my Father which is in heaven, the same is my brother, and sister, and mother."

Notice the word "whosoever". Marvel at its inclusiveness. It incorporates all those from then till now who are truly Christ's brethren and consequently illuminates the reality of God's Fatherhood. When broken men such as we are – or were – understand the meaning of that, they understand at the same time that God cares for them superlatively. He is restless in the presence of their disability. He has set His love on them in the midst of their ruin. He will chasten them so that they will be saved at last and not lost. He cannot keep them against their will but He will never let them go if they will stay. He may sometimes be angry, but it is for love's sake. "He careth for you." That is the summing up of God's Fatherhood. "He careth for you" because you are His and you have been born into the relationship. True fatherhood means begetting a child. You have been begotten of God without any trace of a doubt. "Our Father" expresses the truth as much as any word in this holy revelation.

"Hallowed be thy name"
This is a large subject, too detailed for analysis at this stage. Think of the holy name of Yahweh, Lord of Israel. How do you hallow that holy name? To the people of Israel it was so holy that they would not dare to speak it. We do not have that kind of restraint. How do you hallow that holy name? By singing songs? That can certainly be an expression of reverence and worship, but we have to face the fact that the song may not reach any higher than the ceiling, unless the life corresponds with the dedication of the song.

The truth is that hallowing the name in the deepest sense means living in accordance with those things which the name reveals. I would love to go into that – the deep and wonderful things the name reveals – but now is not the time. It will have to be sufficient to say that the name Yahweh stands most powerfully for the idea of essential being, essential life, abiding, timeless, dateless, infinite – and here is the important thing from the point of view of the context of the pattern prayer.

Yahweh is part of the verb which is used when essential being is declared but it suggests, not only the essential being of God, but the adaption of His being to some necessity. That is why our brethren who understand these things well have expounded the name to mean, "I will be that I will be". In other words, God is revealed as a 'becoming' God – becoming in the sense of being revealed and manifested in others, but as well, becoming to those others all that they need. It stresses the all-sufficiency of God, but more, the all-sufficiency of God active on behalf of others. So from the lips of Abraham, feeling for the truth, there fell the words, "Yahweh Yireh". The 'becoming' one sees and provides: God will provide Himself a Lamb.

So later on the name is interpreted and unveiled in the experience of the Hebrew people. The point I am wanting to stress now is that in this prayer, the holy name of God, the I am – the 'becoming' one, becoming all that His people need, the one who sees and provides, the one with vision and provision – is the one whose name must be hallowed by a sincere response to its deepest implications. "Hallowed be thy name."

Some people have criticised the pattern prayer because on the face of it there seems to be no mention of thanksgiving, which rightly is regarded as an essential part of prayer to God. But hallowing the name of the 'becoming' one calls for the deepest expression of thanksgiving. How can we respond to the one who sees and provides, save by a deep and grateful expression of thanks for His care and carefulness? How can we respond to the one who has given, save by striving to use His gifts in the orbit of His will and never in opposition to it? How can we co-operate with Him in the blessed purpose of being manifested in others, if we nurse in our lives the very things which make manifestation impossible? How can we hallow that holy name if we neglect the holy word wherein that name and all its holy meaning is enshrined and revealed?

Jesus once prayed to his Father for those who were God's other children and he said this:

"I have *manifested thy name* unto the men which thou gavest me out of the world: thine they were, and thou gavest them me; and they have kept thy word."   (John 17:6)

Manifesting the name is not just a matter of using it and singing songs – it is living in accordance with the truth which that holy name exposes and which was made flesh in the one who said: "Before Abraham was, I am."

"Thy kingdom come"

"Our Father which art in heaven, Hallowed be thy name. Thy kingdom come. Thy will be done, as in heaven, so on earth."
It is at the centre of our faith. It is the pole star of all our hopes. It illuminates every dark cloud. It soothes every bereavement, it comforts every sorrow, it alleviates every anxiety – the coming of the King and his blessed kingdom.

Think first of *peace*. Sometimes we think of peace as the absence of war, but it is an impoverished definition. When I was at school they asked me to define heat and I said it was the absence of cold. Then they asked me to define cold and I said it was the absence of heat. They said I should never be a genius! Peace in the noblest sense is that condition where the causes of fear and restlessness and friction are altogether excluded. The Bible gives us the true definition:

"Behold, a king shall reign in righteousness, and princes shall rule in judgement ... and the work of righteousness shall be peace; and the effect of righteousness quietness and assurance for ever. And my people shall dwell in a peaceable habitation, and in sure dwellings, and in quiet resting places."

(Isaiah 32:1,17,18)

That condition of assurance is the very highest quality of true peace – a quality which cannot be shaken.

Sometimes people are inclined to laugh at that picture which the Bible paints of a man sitting under his own fig tree with none making him afraid, but notwithstanding, it has in it the very essence of real peace – that is the absence of fear and the presence of confidence. Make the comparison with now. No longer will men fear the jackboot, the secret police, the brainwashers. No longer man battling with his brother man for territory, for commerce, for selfish advancement. No longer the feverish restless rat race which corrupts and degrades. No longer the noise of strife and battle. No longer the paralysing fear of nuclear bombs. No longer the hopelessness of broken, starving humanity. Instead across the nations and continents, the war mad, strife dominated, fear filled – there comes the song and balm of infinite unshakable peace. All the things which hurt and harm humanity are excluded and banished: man at peace with himself, with nature, and with God.

"How beautiful upon the mountains are the feet of him that bringeth good tidings, that publisheth peace; that bringeth good tidings of good, that publisheth salvation; that saith unto Zion, Thy God reigneth!"   (Isaiah 52:7)

This is the peace that is given by the Lord of Hosts.

Think next of *purity*. Purity is symbolised by the purity of a little child. When the King said: "Suffer little children to come unto me and forbid them not, for of such is the kingdom of heaven", he was alluding, among other things, to the purity of children. The most poetic and inspiring description of the purity of the kingdom of God is in Zechariah chapter 8 – remember, "the city shall be full of boys and girls playing in the streets thereof". That is the purity and safety of the kingdom which enables boys and girls to play together in the streets in perfect safety. Make the comparison with now and you will see what I mean. No perverts, no prostitutes, no degradation, no mugging, no stalking evil. All the Millennial references to children in the Bible are children at play.

"The sucking child shall play on the hole of the asp, and the weaned child shall put his hand on the basilisk's den; the wolf shall dwell with the lamb, and the leopard shall lie down with the kid; and the calf and the young lion and the fatling together; and a little child shall lead them."

(see Isaiah 11:6-8, RV)

A child and the animals are at play.

When I was at school, segregation was the order of the day. There was a boys' entrance and a girls' entrance and the idea was that thereby never the twain should meet. I am glad to say that the great design did not succeed! Today things have changed to some extent, but let us mark it – in the kingdom of God there is no segregation. God's ideal is that manhood and womanhood should be together, because in the conditions which are pure and free from debasement, the strength of manhood makes womanhood strong, and the gentleness of womanhood ennobles manhood. That is why the children are playing together. And then the final revelation is that they are playing in the streets. The streets of the city of Zion are safe for children for, "they shall not hurt nor destroy in all my holy mountain".

So make the comparison and mark the contrast. Mark the great gulf between the city of God and the cities of men. What of our streets today – are they safe for children? In God's city there is perfect safety for the children, and the point is that if the streets are for children, they are fit for everybody. If the streets are safe for the weakest, then they are safe for the strongest. Where the child is safe, everyone is safe. There is nothing to harm, physically, mentally, spiritually. There are no things mechanical to crush young bodies; no things diabolical to pollute young minds. All this is emphasised by Zechariah to stress the purity of the kingdom of God, and to reveal the ideals of the divine government.

Isaiah said once to the people of God – a word for the day when they were ready to leave Babylon and come to Zion – "Be ye clean, that bear the vessels of the LORD" (52:11). And it is men and women such as you, cleansed and purified by the master principles of the kingdom of God, who are to be the ministers of the divine purity in the golden age, establishing a society where the love of purity is greater than the love of gain.

Think finally of *power*. In a shaking world, power of the right kind is like a rock and high tower. The King once said, "All power is given unto me in heaven and in earth". Let us thank God for that assurance. It means that all the diabolical forces of men cannot defeat the enthronement of Jesus the Messiah as King of Zion. And they will try – let us face it. They "shall make war with the Lamb and the Lamb shall overcome them". Because he has submitted to authority he comes to wield it. He is the Prince of Peace and yet he comes with mighty power as a man of war. The authority of the King is the only thing which can halt the power of intoxicated forces of men from their last great act of folly.

As he once arrested the soldiers who came to arrest him, so he will do it again. Judgement is necessary in the interests of peace and purity. The King is at war with the forces which contradict divine purity. He is at war with the paltry tricks of human government which enslave and corrupt those who live in fear. He is at war with the enthronement of mad nationalism and race prejudice. He is at war with those who make money and materialism the only measurement of life. He is at war with those who wantonly use the secret powers of the universe for diabolical purposes. He will speak to the forces which thrive on wickedness with the language of mighty power. His enemies shall lick the dust.

The cowardly booby trappers, the bombers, the terrorists who thrive on fear, the murderers, the torturers – the Lord God of Heaven has so empowered His vice-regal Son that all the forces which hurt and harm humanity are going to be ended by divine power. All nations shall serve him.

Once there fell from His lips a law so perfect and so magnificent that men have said it is unattainable – but at last that law, coming from the wisdom and authority of the King, becomes the perfect law for the final government of humanity. Other rulers consult and amend, or else they make laws which are harsh and despotic. But the King speaks with power, with the voice of supremacy – the final voice, the voice of God. The law of love and purity and divine goodness will be transcendent in every place, and in the very place where the law of men has crumbled to decay. Such is the power of the King and the power of his princes who reign in judgement. They are to be endued with power equal to their high destiny. "To him that overcometh and keepeth my words unto the end, to him will I give power over the nations." So this is what we mean, or ought to mean, when we pray: "Thy kingdom come. Thy will be done, as in heaven, so on earth."

We all now know that the world is groaning. Soon there will be an epidemic of fear. All the burdened multitudes of the world are waiting for a deliverer. It is your destiny and your privilege to bring the healing forces of the kingdom of God to groaning humanity. The world travails, waiting for the manifestation of the Sons of God. That is you! In the power of the Spirit and in the bright radiance of immortality the word of the King is shortly to come true in the fullest sense: "Ye shall be my witnesses ... unto the uttermost part of the earth." So rejoice in it – not boastfully, but tenderly, reverently, thankfully. It is rousing, invigorating, exciting. It is the realisation of all your longing, the issue of all your striving; the satisfaction of all your reverent expectation; the master passion of your faith.

The vision on the distant boundary; the law of love and purity and divine goodness transcendent in the very place where the laws of men have crumbled to decay: such is the power of the King and of the princes who reign in judgement.

The pattern prayer: provision, pardon and protection

THINK first of *provision*. There are some people who believe that when the Lord taught his disciples to pray, "Give us this day our daily bread", he did not mean the bread which is made with flour and baked in the oven. They say he meant the bread of life – the word of God, as though it was too ordinary and earthly a thing to ask the Lord of heaven for baker's bread; as though in some sense the high level of the prayer is demeaned by introducing so base a thing as bread and all the associated things it stands for. Whilst I have the greatest respect for this point of view, I am compelled to say I think it is wrong. I believe that the Lord was teaching us to pray for earthly bread and to do so is truly spiritual. It reveals to us that in the life of faith there is a sacredness of all things which are natural. All natural enjoyments, all natural relationships, are sanctified by the Fatherhood of God.

"Give us this day our daily bread"
All Bible comparisons reveal to us the hidden harmony between the spiritual and the natural. When the Son of God is compared to bread, it is to teach us that he is to us truly and substantially what bread is to us relatively and imperfectly.

When Jesus called himself "the true vine" he was teaching that the vine growing in the field is not false but a wonderful replica of himself. It does imperfectly what he has done to perfection.

Observe then how ordinary things in the family of God become holy. Bread is the gift of God. We call it earthly, but heaven is the birthplace of all earthly gifts. We say that, not to reduce high things to the lowest level, but to endow common things with the grace of God.

Think of Deuteronomy 8:3: "Man doth not live by bread only, but by every word that proceedeth out of the mouth of the LORD doth man live." When it says, "every word that proceedeth out of the mouth of the LORD", it does not mean only the printed word on the parchment of the Bible, but especially that original word which spoke and said, "Let the earth bring forth grass yielding seed" (Genesis 1:11). You see, it is spoken again every seedtime and harvest. We may not hear it but we see the proof of it, thankfully. Bread is the gift of God and He is the provider. Men sometimes blame Him because human incompetence and human greed create hardship where there should be plenty, but when Jesus taught us to pray, "Give us this day our daily bread", he was not leading us to ask for the impossible. Let us understand, we are praying for something which is good and holy and sacred. Observe that the petition comes right next to the kingdom of heaven on earth. The kingdom of God and your daily bread – so earth and heaven are linked in the very centre of the prayer.

"Forgive us our sins"
Think now of *pardon*. Do you not think there is a touch of sadness about that little conjunction 'and' which connects the petition for pardon with the petition for daily bread. You might have expected the conjunction to have been omitted. Could it be there to remind us that as our daily bread comes every day, so do our sins; that as we need to petition each day for our bread and our earthly needs, so we need daily forgiveness. It tells us that the Lord is not only a giver but a forgiver. Jesus once said, "the bread that I will give is my flesh ... for the life of the world". The cost of that giving cannot be calculated in human arithmetic. Pardon is not the only thing which comes to us through the cross of Christ but it is the deepest thing. Every day as we live our lives and see more clearly the absolute purity and utter peace

of the Man of Nazareth, do we also not know more surely the need for pardon? As we know him better is not our conscience more sensitised? At the end of each day, as the sun is westering and our spirits are hushed in the last hour of waking and we ask for his pardon, do we not know that our wounded heart is healed, our withered soul is renewed, our broken humanity is remade? And are we not constrained to thank God for His grace which flows out every day over our life?

One day I came across an old hymn – not one of ours – but I had to admit it expresses what I wanted to say about the plea for pardon. Listen to this – you may know it well, I did not:
"Rock of Ages, cleft for me,
Let me hide myself in thee.
Let the water and the blood
From the riven side which flowed,
Be of sin a double cure –
Save from guilt, and make me pure."
As sin abounded, grace did abound more exceedingly. As we draw near and petition for pardon, there is one tremendous thing we must remember. The High Priest knows us through and through. He knows about the fire in my blood and yours which drives us against our will. He knows how we blundered and did not want to blunder. He has been touched with the feeling of our infirmity. He suffered, being tempted. When we say, 'Our Father, forgive us our trespasses …' we are shut up with the Father and the High Priest of the universe and all other judges are excluded, and we are pardoned and cleansed through the blood of the Lamb and through the amazing mercy of God. In a moment, without delay, as swift as lightning and as gentle as the first breaking of the sunlight, without sign or signal from heaven – no one else is consulted and those who fill their mouths with other men's faults are silenced. The one in need of mercy finds it and is able to lie down to sleep in peace. What a wonderful thing it is, this pardon – and what would our life be like if we could not find it? Let that be the measurement.

"Lead us not into temptation"

Think now of *protection*. The person who is pardoned is striving to avoid recontamination, therefore he prays: "Lead us not into temptation." What is intended by these words could be explained in this way: 'Lord, lead us not where there are snares and pitfalls, for our vision is poor. Lead us not where there are strong enemies, for our strength is impaired. Let not such circumstances as may be for my probation become too powerful for me.' But would the Lord lead a disciple into the occasions of sin? The Bible affirms He would not. God tempts no man, says James. Probably more accurately the petition means, 'Lord, lead me away from temptation'.

There are two kinds of temptation: the temptation to sin and the temptation to refuse sin and do good. When God tempts, He does not tempt men to sin but to do good. Remember the Hebrew man said, "provoking unto love and good works".

God did tempt Abraham, but it was a temptation to engage in a great act of faith. The Bible says categorically that God will not allow His children to be tempted more than they can bear but always will provide a way of escape. Notwithstanding, this is true – God does expose people to situations and circumstances where they will have to declare themselves; that is, where the inwardness is brought out, where people are shown to be externally what they are internally, and secretly.

Judas Iscariot is a case in point. He was made the Lord's treasurer and therefore he was tempted by God to use the Lord's wealth sympathetically, generously and honestly. But he was tempted by his lust to be covetous, mean and dishonest. And he was revealed by the circumstances – his inwardness was brought out.

It was the same with Israel. Remember Deuteronomy 8:2: "The LORD thy God led thee these forty years in the wilderness, to humble thee, and to prove thee, to know what was in thine heart, whether thou wouldest keep his commandments, or no." So the Bible teaches that the grace of God will keep a man from being overwhelmed by temptation, but we should be wrong to think that the grace of God will keep a man if that man is flirting with temptation.

"Lead us not into temptation" implies that we shall flee from it ourselves as, for instance, Joseph did in the house of Potiphar when tempted by Potiphar's wife. It says he "fled and got him out". Jesus counsels us to be wary of it: "Watch and pray that ye enter not into temptation." If it means going the long way round to get home, then go the long way round. Change the books in your bookcase. "Lead us not into temptation" ought to help us to be honest with our timetable and our appetites.

"Deliver us from evil"

Listen to the King praying:

"I pray not that thou shouldest take them out of the world, but that thou shouldest keep them from the evil."

(John 17:15)

The men for whom those words were first spoken were exposed to all kinds of evil, but they were not mastered by it and consequently were delivered from it. So it must be teaching, not that we shall never have to face evil, but rather that we can face it and come through it. We are not immune from danger, or pain or adversity, but because we are the children of our Father whatever happens to us happens within the orbit of His care and in the realm of His control. "All things work together for good to them that love God." If that is not true then the man of Tarsus has deceived us. There is an old saying that the Lord tempers the wind to the shorn lamb – it means that the Lord will change the circumstances for those who need it. This is rarely true. The Lord does not temper the wind to the shorn lamb, but soon gives the lamb a good thick coat to stand against it.

You can take your stand upon the naked word of God:

"[The Lord] hath said, I will never leave thee, nor forsake thee. So that we may boldly say, The Lord is my helper, and I will not fear what man shall do unto me."   (Hebrews 13:5,6)

Moses' words ought to help us. He said, "underneath are the everlasting arms". Underneath means lower than the bottom.

When you are falling through the abyss, Moses says it is into the arms of God. He is your Father. When you say, "deliver us from evil"; when you say, 'I was never lower than this', understand that lower than that, lower than rock bottom, are the loving arms of God. If you think I have overstated it, then tell me what you think Moses meant.

Finally, may I ask you to notice one thing about this pattern prayer. The pronouns: "our", "us", "we". There is not a pronoun in the first person singular. A man may pray it quietly on his own but he cannot pray it alone. As soon as he speaks the words he brings others into his thoughts. When we pray it, we pray with God's other children in our hearts.

Those who first prayed it were once rent by rivalry and strife but at last they were all together "with one accord" in one place. The privileges which were new to them are still with us. We have the same Father, the same High Priest, the same promises. In the pattern prayer every fervent spirit may draw near in worship and every troubled heart may cast its burden on the Lord. Every reverent and hushed spirit may touch the deepest things in the purpose of God. Every soul conscious of its need and receiving so much care and solace may cry out in thankfulness and hallow the blessed name of the 'becoming' one. Every sin-burdened heart may find acquittal and hope. Every weary head may rest here in perfect assurance. Every beleaguered soul may find grace to help in time of need. Every son and daughter may be certified of their place in the family of God.

Upon the pathway of prayer, what a splendid milestone the pattern prayer is.

Public prayer in practice and personal preference

OF all the topics on prayer this is the most difficult, chiefly because it is the most sensitive. How you pray in private nobody knows and any words of mine on private praying will be applied by you or not applied privately.

But with public prayer it is different. Others know how you pray publicly and any words of mine which might comment on public prayer could appear to be commenting on your way of doing it. So you see immediately I am in danger, innocently, of offending you. And that is the very last thing I wish to do. It would grieve me greatly if anything I may say about public prayer seemed that I am getting at somebody. Obviously it is not so because I do not know how you pray in public – but notwithstanding, there is the risk. So may I ask you, please do not feel offended if you have to disagree with what I say. If we are to look at public prayer we have to look at it critically, but we are all in the same boat and have the same faith and want the same end result. You will notice that the title included the words "and personal preference" and that is to stress the point that you cannot provide a straitjacket into which public prayers have to be fitted. How we pray represents our own personality. And this is first-class and should be given full opportunity to be manifested. We may find that if there is a straitjacket it is not personality but tradition. But this we shall discover as we proceed.

First of all there is a kind of public praying which I would like to consider – that is when people gather together in one place especially for prayer. We have done this at my ecclesia at Oxford when we felt a particular need to pray for a special purpose. Recall the words of the King about it:

"Again I say unto you, That if two of you shall agree on earth as touching any thing that they shall ask, it shall be done for them of my Father which is in heaven. For where two or three are gathered together in my name, there am I in the midst of them."   (Matthew 18:19,20)

"Where two or three are gathered ..."
Notice that although one method, the private method, demanded isolation, this method calls for fellowship. Notice very carefully the conditions. The King did not say, 'Where two or three assemble and pray on the basis of their own desire ...' – not that at all. Every word is important: "Where two or three are gathered together in my name ..." The word "gathered" is very significant. It is not the same as 'met together' or 'assembled'. "Gathered" implies that there is a central force which attracts things from the circumference to the centre. The King is the gatherer. Those who come together have been drawn by him because they have been illuminated by his word, impulsed by his love and in the deep recesses of their life are seeking to do his will.

And the king says that where these conditions exist, there he is in the midst. He is in the centre – not hovering at the circumference. He is the centripetal force which holds them together. And if in the spiritual sense he is in the centre of that little company, it means in fact that he is enthroned, obeyed, and consulted, and therefore the prayer should be in harmony with his teaching and according to God's purpose. So the promise made by the King becomes possible and credible.

The answer is assured – but whether it comes in the way we would have expected and at the time we wanted depends on other factors which can be considered under the heading of Unanswered Prayer. According to the King then in this passage, there are limitations upon prayer, but the limitation is not on the things about which we may pray, but upon our own condition and the purpose and spirit in which we make our petition. Of course, the truth is that some people find this kind of public prayer helpful and even inspiring and others find it almost the opposite. Some like it; some dislike it. It shows that personal preference is a factor not to be discounted. Experience has taught me it needs careful planning else it will fail.

Long prayers

A good prayer can be spoilt when it goes on too long, when it repeats itself several times and when the sentences are discerned as padding to run it on longer. How often have you heard the same thing in a prayer repeated several times as though God needed to be pestered or the audience might forget? In an address repetition is often very useful, but a prayer is not an address, or at least it should not be. Long prayers tend to weary people in the congregation who are elderly and find standing difficult and distracting. It spoils the prayer for them because the weariness intrudes into their consciousness too much and they lose their concentration.

You, no doubt, have heard the story of the man who made a long prayer, quoting many passages and eventually getting to Hebrews 11 where he quoted, "... and what more shall we say?" – a weary voice in the congregation said: "Say nowt more – just say Amen!" It may not be true, but if it was, I can understand why.

Here is a prayer so contrived as to be an example:

"O great and eternal Father in heaven, hallowed be thy name. Thy kingdom come. We thank thee that thou hast allowed us to come together once more to show to our friends and neighbours the great things which thou hast promised in thy word which thou hast magnified above thy name and which thou hast vouchsafed to us thy servants.

"We thank thee that thou hast called us out of darkness into thy marvellous light. We rejoice that we are not as the world is – in darkness and sin, and we thank thee that thou hast called us to understand thy will, and to separate us from the things which are worldly and ungodly.

"Grant that those who have turned in tonight to hear thy word and who have not yet responded to the Gospel may not much longer delay their decision, for we know that the time is short and there may not much longer be opportunity to hear and answer the call. For we know that the judgements will soon fall upon those who have neglected thy truth and spurned thy offer of salvation. Call them we beseech thee to baptism and obedience while there is yet time.

"We thank thee that thou hast revealed to us thy purpose with this earth and man upon it and for the assurance that we need not suffer the fate of Adamic stock.

"We pray for the peace of Jerusalem, for until she is at peace there will be no peace in our hearts.

"We are mindful of those who are on beds of sickness – whether it be of mind or of body and ask thee to let thy healing hand rest upon them.

"Thou the God of Abraham, Isaac and Jacob, in whom is no change or shadow cast by turning, and whom not having seen we love, whom to know is eternal life, grant us a humble place in thy kingdom and pardon us for the things which we ought to have done and left undone and those things which we have done which we ought never to have done.

"Hear us in heaven, thy dwelling place and let thy blessing be upon us as we further wait upon thee. We ask it in the name of Jesus and for his sake. Amen."

Not a bad prayer and it does express the feelings and faith of many of us, nay all of us. But I think it could be improved. It does tend to be wordy and some of the phrases are well-worn and very traditional. There were many petitions and some of the sentences were quite evidently designed to be addressed to the visitors rather than to God. It was a kind of mini exhortation for the hesitating strangers. It was certainly rather long for a public meeting. I hope it will not cause offence if I say that there are some things about it which could be left out, or, if left in, could be changed.

There really is no need for people who are ill always to be on 'beds of sickness', or to refer to the world as 'this earth and man upon it'. You know what I mean – there is no need to amplify it. The prayer which is wordy, full of archaic phrases, with many petitions and references is going to be too long. Is such a prayer really suitable for a public meeting?

The memorial service
Talking about being suitable – I beg to say a few words about prayers at the breaking of bread service; that is, giving thanks for the emblems. There is a proper way to do this and it is often disregarded. First of all, these prayers should not be long. Then they should be related to the particular emblem rightly.

The prayer for the bread should give thanks for the body of Christ and the loving sacrifice which was made by the Son when he offered his body on the tree.

The prayer for the wine should give thanks for the shed blood, shed for the remission of sins and should always include a plea for pardon for sins. This is the duty of the brother who gives thanks for the wine – the plea for pardon – not for the brother who gives thanks for the bread. Sometimes this procedure is ignored and the bread prayer has a strong plea for forgiveness, and the poor man who has to give thanks for the wine has been robbed of the main purpose of his prayer.

On Sundays in our services the main prayer is that offered in the memorial service by the presiding brother. This should be a comprehensive prayer, offering worship, thanksgiving and praise; seeking blessing and help and guidance. It should remember the sick, the bereaved, those in special need; it should pray for the coming of the kingdom, the return of the absent Lord, the blessing of the ecclesia; it should pray for those in authority, for the chosen people; it should thank God for His word and for the word made flesh, for the great atoning plan of redemption. It need not be very long but it should remember to be comprehensive because it is the main prayer of the day.

One more point is this. Public prayer can sometimes be without life. It can be cold and decorous and formal in a way that robs it of appeal, or inspiration. When you pray in public, pray with feeling, pray with warmth, pray with faith, and make it clear that you believe what you are saying. Nothing is worse than to sound in your praying as if you are bored. I know you are not of course, but we must never give the impression that we might be. And if your voice trembles sometimes, fear not – God loves prayers that are fervent.

Prayers addressed to Jesus

I come now to something which might be profitable to ponder and it is this. Sometimes in public prayer, brethren pray directly to Jesus. It may not happen often but when it does it can be a problem. The first point is that if it is going to disturb the assent and tranquility of others, then it does not help the unity of the prayer forward.

But allowing that – to what extent is it theologically right and ought anyone to engage in it publicly? Those who do it justify it on the grounds that there are in the New Testament prayers offered to Jesus Christ specifically. The examples are when Paul says about his thorn in the flesh: "I besought the Lord thrice, that it might depart from me. And he said unto me, My grace is sufficient for thee" (2 Corinthians 12:8,9).

Then there is Paul's prayer of thanks: "I thank Christ Jesus our Lord, who hath enabled me, for that he counted me faithful, putting me into the ministry" (1 Timothy 1:12).

Then there is the case of the apostles choosing a new apostle to replace Judas: "They prayed and said, Thou Lord, which knoweth the hearts of all men, shew whether of these two thou hast chosen, that he may take part of this ministry and apostleship ..." (Acts 1:24,25).

Then other references in Acts. First the case of the martyrdom of Stephen in Acts 7:59. Stephen called upon God saying, "Lord Jesus, receive my spirit".

Paul on the Damascus Road in Acts 9 when struck to the ground heard the voice of Jesus, and he said, "Who art thou, Lord?" And the Lord said, "I am Jesus whom thou persecutest".

Peter on the roof top in Acts 10 saw a vision and a voice said, "Rise, Peter; kill, and eat". Peter said, "Not so, Lord; for I have never eaten anything that is common or unclean".

There are two other references but they are of Paul recounting his experience on the Damascus Road and therefore repeating what he said to Jesus and what Jesus said to him.

So that is the case. My view of it tells me that all these incidents were very special and very personal and in some cases those concerned, having been spoken to by Jesus, had of necessity to reply to him. In the case of Stephen it was the response to a vision of Christ. In the case of Peter, again it was in response to a vision. In the case of the selection of a new apostle, it was the need to ask for guidance. The point is that all these cases were special cases, peculiar to unusual circumstances. I am not convinced that they are telling us what the normal procedure should be for later times.

In the New Testament, prayers to Jesus, as we understand prayer, do not occur. As a regular normal thing they are quite definitely not there. Furthermore, the teaching of Jesus was that men should pray to the Father in heaven through the Son – through the name of Jesus. This was to be the normal method of praying. For example:

"And whatsoever ye shall ask in my name, that will I do, that the Father may be glorified in the Son. If ye shall ask any thing in my name, I will do it."   (John 14:13,14)

"Ye have not chosen me, but I have chosen you, and ordained you, that ye should go and bring forth fruit, and that your fruit should remain: that whatsoever ye shall ask of the Father in my name, he may give it you."   (15:16)

"And in that day ye shall ask me nothing. Verily, verily, I say unto you, Whatsoever ye shall ask the Father in my name, he will give it you."   (16:23)

That is pretty clear instruction about praying and it is the counsel of Jesus himself. We honour his name by doing his will. He did not say, 'Ask me and I will do it'. He said, 'Ask my Father in my name, and he will do it'. To say this is how we ought to pray is not to dishonour the Son or to diminish in any way his glory.

The great majority of brethren and sisters hold this view of it and, therefore, to introduce into public prayer what must be an innovation, is something which is not likely to benefit those who wish to say the 'Amen'. What disciples do in their private prayer about this is something their own conviction must decide, but we are concerned in this section about public prayer.

Prayer in communal worship

Finally, I would like to stress the part that public prayer has to play in the quality of communal worship. I think we must all have been conscious of this when prayer has in a wonderful way enhanced the quality of that worship – and perhaps, sadly, when it has impaired it. It does show what a serious thing it is to offer public prayer, and indeed what an inspiring opportunity it gives to gather together the minds and hearts of your comrades in the faith and present them before the Lord of the universe. When we think of the meaning of worship, the essential element in the word is that of reverence. The idea is that of being prostrate, of walking out backwards, of obeisance. It is a reverent recognition of the utter superiority of God. It is an admission that the throne of God is the holy place of the universe and that in the presence of the throne, men must bow and submit. Worship involves also a recognition that man is absolutely dependent on God for all things; a confession that all the needs of life are to be found and satisfied in the God of heaven. Worship enforces on the mind of man that he is altogether incomplete and wasted apart from his Creator. A sense of man's need and God's sufficiency is at the very heart of true worship. The attitude of worship is the attitude of a subject bent before the king. Or the attitude of a sheep following the shepherd, and being content and satisfied with the pasture which is appointed by the shepherd.

So I am stressing that it is this spirit which should inspire public prayer. Reverence and godly fear is the foundation. I think in every way in our worship we should strive for reverence, and our prayers can point the way powerfully. How compelling are the words of prayer that tell of the greatness and power of the Creator and Sustainer of all life; the syllables of praise that tell of the goodness and grace and the all-sufficiency of the Father of those who are His children; the sentences which confess that in proportion as our life is abandoned to Him, we shall find peace and joy.

The last thing just now about public prayer to remark on is this – the discipline which it enforces upon us or should enforce upon us. This is what I mean. Your brethren and sisters hear the words you speak and they will expect the words to be sincere, that is, what you speak will correspond as far as possible with how you are. If it does not, then there is a strong likelihood that the prayer will lose its impact as far as the assembly is concerned.

Let me illustrate: if somebody says in his prayer what a wonderful privilege it is to be at the memorial service but he only comes when he is presiding, then the words seem empty. Or if I thank God for the wonderful blessing of His living word in the Bible, but they know that I hardly ever look at it and never come when it is being expounded – then the syllables I have spoken carry little weight.

So this is what I mean. Public prayer is a powerful force to make us more instant upon being like we say we want to be in the prayer we offer. It just emphasises that sincerity is a vital element in the ministry of praying in public. Of course, we all fall short of it. Our aspirations are always better than our achievements, but let us recognise it and take courage.

Prayer problems
Romans 8

THINK what we mean by prayer problems. We mean the difficulties, doubts, impediments which halt and hinder progress along the pathway of prayer. There is no doubt that problems do exist and it is not surprising in such a personal subject as prayer. Then again, sometimes it is a matter of practice – how to put into practice the teaching which we have learned and understood. Of course, what is a problem to one person is not to another. What baffles you would not baffle your neighbour. It is often a matter of trying to make sense of some of the things which are revealed about prayer. Let us be honest – some things are not easy to grasp fully in these days. They were right for the infant church, but are they right for us?

It is one thing to approve a principle, it is sometimes another thing to realise in the commonplaces of daily life. The problems we are to consider in this section are those which have come to notice in our experience, and we hope that any problems you may have will be covered, at least in part.

So, let us come now to prayer problems.

Praying – and a shortage of words
Sometimes it is said that when praying, after a short time, there is nothing more to say; there is a shortage of thoughts or a shortage of words – our petitions and our thanksgiving are quickly exhausted. I must confess that this is one of my problems. It is not easy to keep praying for, say, fifteen minutes. If you will pardon me for making a personal reference, when

I was a young man in the church of Rome there was what was called the *Quarant Ore* – that is forty hours of prayer. We had to put our names down for the particular hour we would watch in prayer. The young men were expected to do it through the night – I used to go say from 2 am to 3 am. I found it very difficult to keep praying for an hour. I used to take a book of prayers of the saints and read them. I find the same difficulty today.

Of course, it may not be needful to pray for a long time: perhaps ten minutes is enough time to speak all you have to say. But there are people who worry over this and when they have the time they feel they ought to pray for longer. If you are one of those, then the idea I have referred to already may still be helpful, though in this case not a book of the church saints' prayers but the book of God, His holy word. Have the word of God before you when you pray.

The idea is to read a portion, then meditate upon it for a while and then pray, then read again. In this way new thoughts are provoked, new feelings, new ideas which can be converted into prayer. If you feel this appeals to you then the part of the Bible which is most profitable is, of course, the Psalms. They have a way of putting into words some of the inmost thoughts of the soul and mind, which perhaps without the aid of the Psalms would remain inarticulate. It is possible to take the words of the Psalmist and incorporate them into our own prayers and petitions and feel them to be deeply true for our own experience and our own needs.

If you feel sad and forsaken in some way, then have Isaiah 41 before you when you pray. I once knew a man who always felt sad on a Monday for personal reasons: he always had Psalm 116 before him when he prayed on that day. I heard of one sister who found Revelation 5 a good chapter to use in prayer as it lured her on to think about the glory of God.

Paul said, "I will pray with the understanding also", and there are disciples who say that having the word of God open when praying gives more understanding to their prayers. I leave it to you to ponder. It may not be everybody's way of dealing with this problem of a shortage of words, but it is a suggestion, if you have time.

A problem allied to this matter of a shortage of words is having to use the same words, day after day. Again this is a problem with me – saying the same things day after day with the same words. Of course I do try to vary as much as I can, but there are limits to the variations that can be applied. There are only a limited number of ways in which you can express thanks for gifts and benefits and for the great gift of redemption. How many ways can you pray for the coming of the kingdom? Then, of course, having to confess the same failures every day reinforces the problem of sameness.

Now I think we just have to face the facts that as far as God is concerned it does not matter. It seems to matter to us but we must believe that in God's sight it is not important. Our Heavenly Father does not mind if we use the same sentences day after day. Although it may worry us, the lack of vocabulary is not a problem in heaven. After all, it is not the eloquence which commends the prayer to God but the inward spirit which prompts it. Do not misunderstand me, I have nothing against a prayer spoken beautifully with moving sentences. Indeed, for public prayer it can be a great help, but for private prayer it is not essential. Of course, using the same words time after time, we must be careful that it does not become just a performance, a repetition with no purpose. That is a danger in repetition but we must guard against it when we use the same words regularly. If the heart is truly in it then the spirit of the prayer will transcend the actual words and it is this that matters.

Unanswered prayer
There ought to be no doubt in our minds that God does answer prayer. Assurances abound in the Bible that this is true. Christ's own words are precise and emphatic: "Every one that asketh receiveth" (Matthew 7:8). He taught us to pray for the forgiveness of sins and for daily bread. He would never have taught us thus if there were no answers to prayer. But we must be honest and

recognise that there are conditions and limitations. Prayers that lack faith and sincerity are not heard. God judges by the heart and we approve of that kind of judgement. Given the right conditions on our side, there are sometimes situations where God does not grant us what we ask. We ought not to suppose that the prayer is unanswered or that God is indifferent. As has been said before – 'No' is an answer. Good men have had to hear the answer 'No'. Moses prayed that he might go over Jordan, but he did not. Elijah prayed that he might die, but he did not. Paul prayed for the removal of his affliction, but it did not come. These three are great men of God in the Bible and yet their requests were not granted, but the prayers were answered.

In each case there were good reasons why God did not grant the request at once. We must remember that delays are not denials. It is better to await God's time because He can see the end from the beginning, and we can never do that. Moses did not get into Canaan, but he will one day and in the finest sense of all – to stay. Elijah did not die for loneliness and God showed him instead that there were seven thousand in Israel who had taken his God to be their God. God made him live to see the triumph of his life – the unsurmised obedience of seven thousand faithful souls in the midst of Israel. Paul kept his thorn in the flesh and when he understood its purpose he would not be without it. His weakness was made perfect in God's strength. God may refuse our way and our route because He knows a better one. Sometimes we cry for things which are unsuitable, unsafe, and unwise. More than once people have lived to thank God that He withstood their agonised entreaties and refused their earnest prayers for something which at the time seemed indispensable, but which retrospectively was seen to be a curse.

God always has a reason for refusal. He knows better than we do. He can see our characters and knows that there are reasons which must sometimes disqualify us from receiving something with which others are safe. He knows that the immediate may imperil the future. Have you ever thought that God gave Hezekiah fifteen years extra to his life, and when you look at them it does seem he would have been much better without them. Brother Len Richardson once said: "Be careful what you ask for – you may get it." Ponder it and learn a lesson about prayer.

Praying for somebody else
This is a problem for some people because they are inclined to argue that however much you may pray for certain things to happen to somebody else, it cannot happen unless they themselves are willing for it to happen. You cannot pray for the recovery of someone from sin unless they themselves are willing to repent. It would not be fair for God to make them do what you ask against their will, so is it right to pray for other people? Is it asking God for something which is impossible? Will God bless someone else at my request if they themselves are indifferent? Now when you look at the Bible it is soon evident that whatever problems may arise there is a good case for praying for other people. There is a good case for being an intercessor.

Think of the examples: Job prayed for his children; Abraham pleaded for Sodom. Surely that is an excellent argument for praying for what seems a hopeless situation. Moses made intercession for Israel; David prayed for the people he ruled; Samuel prayed all night for Saul; Daniel prayed for the deliverance of the people of God.

You would never think that God is taken by surprise, but here is a strange thing: the one thing that is said to have surprised God – can you remember it? "And [God] saw that there was no man, and wondered that there was no intercessor" (Isaiah 59:16). Or again the same idea in Ezekiel: "And I sought for a man among them, that they should make up the hedge, and stand in the gap before me for the land, that I should not destroy it: but I found none" (22:30). So it looks as though it is something normal to intercede for others.

It seems that prayer may well be private but it is never solitary. It ought to be personal but it cannot be isolated: "None of us liveth to himself" (Romans 14:7). The life we live is relative and always interdependent. Praying, like life, is vicarious. That one lonely man who is the Saviour of the world – of him it is said: "He bare the sin of many, and made intercession for the transgressors" (Isaiah 53:12). Isaiah and Daniel identified themselves with the people they led. Think of the father of the epileptic boy, and the despairing mother of the demon-possessed girl. In each case they prayed for another and were heard.

One way of bearing the burden of others is praying for them that they may place themselves in a position where God can remove the burden and ease the agony or cleanse the pollution. There are difficulties no doubt, but faith ventures hopefully upon the promises of God and trusts God to blow away the chaff and keep the grain.

The Spirit helping our infirmities
Think of the material sentence:
"Likewise the Spirit also helpeth our infirmities: for we know not what we should pray for as we ought: but the Spirit itself maketh intercession for us with groanings which cannot be uttered. And he that searcheth the hearts knoweth what is the mind of the Spirit, because he maketh intercession for the saints according to the will of God."   (Romans 8:26,27)
The problem here is knowing exactly what Paul meant by these words. I think we can say without any doubt what he did not mean. He is not saying that the Holy Spirit, the third person of the Trinity, a person separate from God the Father, takes our imperfect prayers, and groaning in an inarticulate and distressing way somehow presents them to God. If anyone believes in the Trinity that might make some sense, but it still raises the difficulty about the Holy Spirit being God Himself, being in a state of inarticulation, groaning and sighing. It is difficult to imagine this to be true of the Deity Himself.

I came across an interesting passage in Grimm-Thayer's *Lexicon* about this verse, and quote it as follows:
"The phrase 'the spirit intercedes with unutterable groanings' [in Romans 8:26] means, as the whole context shows, nothing other than this: 'Although we have no very definite conception

of what we desire, and cannot state it in fit language in our prayer but only disclose it by inarticulate groanings, yet God receives these groanings as acceptable prayers inasmuch as they come from a soul full of the Holy Spirit'."

We should have difficulty in agreeing with that final phrase, yet it does present the passage in a way which makes it understandable. I suggest to be consistent we ought to understand the word "Spirit" in this passage in the way we interpret it in the earlier part of the chapter. In verse 1 we understand the words, "walk not after the flesh, but after the Spirit", to mean, 'refusing the domination of the natural appetite we live in accordance with the spiritual principles which have been revealed by God's Holy Spirit in His word'. The definition is clearly marked in verses 5 and 6:

"For they that are after the flesh do mind the things of the flesh; but they that are after the Spirit the things of the Spirit. For to be carnally minded is death; but to be spiritually minded is life and peace."

To be fair, the word "spirit" is synonymous with being spiritually-minded, which is another way of expressing what the New Testament calls the "new man" – the born again nature, created in holiness and righteousness by the word of the living God.

This is how Brother John Carter sees it in his book, *The Letter to the Romans*. I now quote from that work about this verse:

"The 'new man' when in suffering, approaches the Father in prayer. But for what shall he pray? For the suffering to be removed? Or for strength to endure? In his groaning he asks, after the example of Jesus, 'Now is my soul troubled: and what shall I say? Father, save me from this hour. But for this cause came I unto this hour. Father, glorify thy name' (John 12:27,28). 'O my Father, if it be possible, let this cup pass from me; nevertheless not as I will, but as thou wilt' (Matthew 26:39). 'And he that searcheth the hearts knoweth what is the mind of the Spirit, that he maketh intercession for the saints according to the will of God.'"

(1992 edition, page 100)

So he is saying that the new man is the spirit which, although encumbered by the weakness of the flesh, is able to express through groaning and grieving, albeit weakly, the things that are desired, and the one who is able to search the hearts is able to discern what the spirit, the new man, really is seeking.

It is my opinion that we shall find help in understanding this if we remember the known facts as they are revealed in the word of God. These for example:

"For there is one God, and one mediator between God and men, the man Christ Jesus."   (1 Timothy 2:5)

"But this man, because he continueth ever, hath an unchangeable priesthood. Wherefore he is able also to save them to the uttermost that come unto God through him, seeing he ever liveth to make intercession for them."   (Hebrews 7:24,25)

"For Christ is not entered into the holy places made with hands, which are the figures of the true, but into heaven itself, now to appear in the presence of God for us."   (9:24)

"Who is he that condemneth? It is Christ that died, yea rather that is risen again, who is even at the right hand of God, who also maketh intercession for us."   (Romans 8:34)

"For we have not an high priest which cannot be touched with the feeling of our infirmities; but was in all points tempted like as we are, yet without sin."   (Hebrews 4:15)

Now all those passages insist on one thing – that the intercessor at the throne of God is Jesus, the High Priest.

In Romans 8:26 it says that "the Spirit itself maketh intercession for us". But we know that the Spirit is not a person, it is a power. Furthermore we know without the slightest doubt that it is the Christ who makes intercession for us. So I incline to the simple explanation. The Spirit here in Romans 8 is in fact the High Priest, the one mediator, the sympathetic intercessor who has been touched with our infirmity and can therefore understand our weakness.

It means therefore, as I understand it, that the Lord Jesus himself, through his Holy Spirit, presents to God the Father the imperfect prayers of the saints. He takes the prayers as they are, chaff and grain together, and with the breath of kindness and sympathetic understanding, blows away the chaff and puts before his Father the grain.

It ought not to surprise us that the activity of the High Priest is presented to us as the work of the Spirit. In several ways the Holy Spirit was active in the infant church, but it was in fact the head of the church who was acting. The Spirit says: "Separate me Barnabas and Saul", but it was the Christ who said it because he is the head of the ecclesia of God in the world.

"After they were come to Mysia, they assayed to go into Bithynia; but the Spirit suffered them not."   (Acts 16:7) You can be sure it was the head of the ecclesia who "suffered them not" – communicating through the Holy Spirit.

Jesus said, "All power is given unto me in heaven and in earth". We believe that the Spirit is the power of God and the Spirit is at the command of the one who sits on the right hand of the throne in heaven. You may be interested to know that in that sentence from Acts 16:7 just quoted, it says, "the Spirit of Jesus suffered them not" (see RV). That is just my case: the Spirit which intercedes is the Spirit of Jesus – the power at his disposal – quick on behalf of the stumbling voices of the saints.

I think we have to face the fact that human nature being what it is we pray sometimes for wrong things. Naturally we pray for the things we regard as the most urgent and nobody can complain about that, but we have to admit that the most urgent from our point of view may not be the most important from God's point of view. Measured by our own desire we would like good health, home comfort, happiness and reasonable success. Measured by God's standard these things may not always be a blessing, and may sometimes be a hindrance.

Sometimes those who have asked God to prolong the life of another have lived to thank Him that He did not. So we have to confess that standing by ourselves we do not know what we should pray for as we ought. But there is help when the new man is our aid – the new spiritual mind created and nurtured by the Spirit. It means the development of the mind and heart to understand the wisdom of God in the realm of prayer, that is to create in the saints the right conditions for praying rightly. It is being led by the Spirit. Remember, Jesus said about the Spirit, "He shall take of mine, and shall shew it unto you" (John 16:15) – the revelation of the Spirit of Christ. So bit by bit, under the influence of the Spirit, in the Spirit's word we learn to pray more nearly in accordance with the Lord's will.

Walking in the Spirit means walking in accordance with the things which are spiritual – so praying in the Spirit means praying in accordance with that which is truly spiritual and therefore in accordance with God's will. We must never forget the place of the advocate in heaven in this process. There is, as it appears to me, a kind of unity of intercession between the High Priest in heaven and the spiritual new man in the praying soul, as though what is prayed imperfectly with groanings by the intercessor on earth, is prayed again more perfectly by the intercessor in heaven, so that in a certain sense the two become one. The imperfect groaning is our imperfect humanity with all its limitations, but that groaning finds true expression in the intercession of the High Priest at the throne of God. He saves those, "that come unto God through him, seeing he ever liveth to make intercession for them" (Hebrews 7:25). The intercession is twofold. The High Priest cannot present the plea of the prayer which is dominated by an unyielding will. The pure in heart may see God. The carnal mind is not in tune with the Spirit. The pathway demands willing submission to the principles of prevailing prayer.

Obviously it does not come overnight – it is not magic, but it is like fruit: it develops as the life expands. As our discipleship gets more truly spiritual so our praying will get more spiritual. Of course I must say that there are good faithful Bible students, better equipped than I am, who would have a different explanation for Romans 8 – but a man has to speak in harmony with his conviction.

Those not in the Truth seem to get answers to prayer
This may not be a problem with you but it is with some people. One way of answering it is to deny it, but that is no help to those who are worried by it.

Let me give you example of what I mean. Years ago there was a man living in Bristol and his name was George Muller. He was a Christian: probably what Brother Thomas would call a misbeliever – not an unbeliever but a misbeliever. Insofar as his knowledge went, he was a man of great faith. He had one compelling way of life, to be a father to two hundred orphaned children; that is to say, he ran an orphanage. He had no source of income for the work save that which was donated by good men and women who were moved to help him.

Now many times he was at his wits' end to know where the next meal was to come from. One night when all was settled down, he confessed to a visitor he had staying with him to help that there was nothing for the next day's breakfast. So George Muller and his friend simply went to praying and laid their problem before the Lord, earnestly. Then they went to bed. Before dawn they were awakened by a knocking at the front door. There was a van driver hammering at the door and he had with him a van load of bread with an explanation that somehow something had gone wrong with the baking arrangements that night and they had badly miscalculated – they had a load of bread they could not sell and would Mr. Muller like it for the children. The story is so well authenticated by reliable witnesses, people of undoubted integrity, and it would be churlish to make them all foolish dreamers or at worst all liars and deceivers, just to get ourselves out of a difficulty.

I have an explanation which for my own soul's sake keeps my spirit at rest. First of all I do not know at what level of knowledge people become responsible to God. I do not think it is a static thing; it varies from situation to situation. Therefore I cannot, or dare not say when God will answer the prayers of other people who are not in the Truth as we are. This is no criticism of any who feel they can say when God will answer. So I do not know how responsible George Muller was with God.

But there is something else. I believe that God is related to men on two levels. One I call related providentially and the other related salvationally. Because He is the Creator of all men, He is in a sense the Father of all men – what might be called the Creative Fatherhood. In the words quoted by Paul in Acts 17, "We are all his offspring". The Bible tells us that God cares providentially for His offspring. Jesus said He makes His sun to shine on the just and the unjust. Paul says in one great inclusive sentence about God's relationship with men: "Nevertheless he left not himself without witness, in that he did good, and gave us rain from heaven, and fruitful seasons, filling our hearts with food and gladness" (Acts 14:17). The brotherhood of man is true in Adam because of the universal Fatherhood of God. Because of this relationship, God cares for men providentially.

On the other hand, God is related to some people salvationally. This is God's redemptive Fatherhood as distinct from His Creative Fatherhood. The point to make now is that under the providential care of God for men, when people in faith seek His help He answers their prayers. He is one God and subjects His will to one law. He is compassionate towards His offspring, and that compassion allows Him to answer the cry of the needy. This may account for the fact that people who are not in covenant relationship with Him as we are, may receive answers to their prayers. It may explain the strange event in Bristol which happened to a man, who being in need, turned to his Creator on behalf of the orphaned and destitute.

Ought children who are not baptized be allowed to pray?
This is a question that has troubled many brethren and sisters over the years, especially those who are parents. There are differing views about it. At the end of his book on prayer called *Making Prayer Powerful*, Brother H. P. Mansfield gives some information about the opinions of our early brethren. Brother Thomas thought that in view of the scriptural conditions that are

attached to acceptable worship, children should not be asked to pray. Brother Robert Roberts thought it permissible for them to do so, provided they understood that their approach to God was simply that of the creature to the Creator.

Sister Roberts has something interesting on children and worship – she says:

"God hears 'the ravens when they cry' (Job 38:41; Psalm 147:9); and, as Paul told the Athenians, 'We are also his offspring'. He has heard the prayers of sinners when it suited His purpose – see Pharaoh. He heard him, and granted Pharaoh's requests. Coming down to New Testament times, there is the Lord's own attitude, when the children greeted him with their Hosannahs! When the Pharisees asked him to rebuke them, he replied that if he did 'the stones would immediately cry out' (Luke 19:40). We teach our children to thank any friend who gives them anything, and should we not teach them to thank God who gives us everything we possess?"   (*Christadelphian Answers*, page 56)

Brother H. P. Mansfield says that God has neither invited prayer from any out of Christ nor directly forbidden it. Let those who follow Brother Roberts' advice take care to heed the qualifications he mentions.

Personally I am very impressed by Mark 10:14 – the case of Jesus being angry when his disciples forbade the children to come to him. He said, "Suffer the little children to come unto me, and forbid them not (do not hinder them, RSV)".

So if we are faced with making a difficult decision about children coming to Jesus, then in striking the balance we should lean to the side which makes it easier for them to come rather than to the side which makes it difficult, because Jesus said, "Do not hinder them".

The New Testament writers insist that Jesus is the same yesterday, today and for ever. It seems to me that a simple mind asking the question today whether children ought to be allowed to pray and looking to see the attitude of Jesus to children, would very much gain the impression that Christ was glad to receive the approach and the words of children – and that would strengthen the conviction that the Father of Jesus would be willing to receive their approach and their words in prayer.

I say, different people have differing views and I think we must be tolerant of those who may not agree with us on this subject, whichever way it is.

BOOK THREE
Matthew's Messiah

Immanuel and Jesus
Matthew 1 and 2

B Y way of introduction there are three points we wish to
emphasise. Firstly, this is not a verse by verse study of
the Gospel of Matthew. That would be a very interesting
exercise upon another occasion, but it is not the purpose of this
exercise. In this study we are concerned to notice certain aspects
of Matthew's conception of the Messiah. Put another way, we
wish to mark how the Holy Spirit used Matthew's mind and
spirit to present an insight into the person of the Messiah and
his mission. So to understand it rightly, this is not a complete
study but a kind of thematic selection from Matthew's Gospel of
certain insights into the Hebrew Messiah.

Secondly, although it is Matthew's vision we are concerned
with, I would like to look at the other Gospel writers when it is
necessary. It may well be that Matthew can be illuminated by a
reference to Mark, Luke or John. So, give me that licence and do
not hold me exclusively to Matthew.

Thirdly, you will understand that the method of approach
will not be chronological. Being concerned with distinct themes
we shall go where the themes emerge and where they develop.
So in one minute we may be at the beginning of the Gospel and
the next, at the end. To students of God's word this will come as
no surprise.

Having said that, let us begin at the beginning:
"The book of the generation of Jesus Christ, the son of David,
the son of Abraham."   (Matthew 1:1)

The genealogy

It is not likely that Matthew meant that his whole Gospel was "the book of the generation of Jesus Christ" – these words are more likely meant to apply to the verses which describe the record of the genealogy of Jesus Christ as Matthew has taken it from the Hebrew records, to prove that this Jesus has descended from Abraham and from David.

If that was his purpose, the first thing we must remark on is that really it failed to prove this. It proves very conclusively that *Joseph* descended from Abraham and David, but as Joseph was not the father of Jesus, it really cannot authenticate the descent of Jesus through the male line from Abraham and David.

Let me give you an up to date illustration of this problem. There was once a man named Robert Stuart and he was a direct descendant in the male line from James Stuart, James VI of Scotland who, as you may know, became James I of England in 1603. Robert married a young widow named Mary Anderson. She already had a boy of two years of age by her first husband, Roy Anderson. When she married Robert Stuart, the boy's name was changed to Alex Stuart from Alex Anderson. Eventually, Mary Stuart (née Anderson) sought to prove that her son Alex was a direct descendant of the royal Stuart line – she wanted to say that her son descended from James I, not only legally but genetically. It was a hopeless aspiration. In the court it was proved beyond doubt that Robert Stuart was not the father of the child and that the real father, Roy Anderson, had no blood relationship with the Stuart line. The claim failed on this point and Mary Anderson's hopes were dashed.

Now this is a good illustration of the problem arising from the genealogy in Matthew chapter 1. Joseph was a genuine descendant through the male line from Abraham and David, but he was not the father of Jesus. Notice the change in verse 16: "And Jacob *begat* Joseph the husband of Mary, of whom *was born* Jesus, who is called Christ." The words "and he begat" are left out and instead we have "of whom was born Jesus". He does not say that Joseph begat Jesus, but that he was Mary's husband, and she bore the child Jesus. This of course is in harmony with the virgin birth of the child.

But the question that faces us is this: What then was the purpose of this genealogy, since strictly speaking it cannot prove the descent of Jesus on the male side? Why did Matthew begin his Gospel with this evidence? What does it prove? What was its purpose? It is probably this. Matthew, measuring the attitude of the Hebrews towards the case of Jesus, judged it to be important to show that Joseph, on the human level the only attributable father, was a direct descendant of Abraham and David. Put another way, if Joseph had been of the tribe of, say, Dan, so would Jesus according to the Hebrews. In the Hebrew mind it would not have been sufficient to prove fleshly descent from a *mother* of David's line as legal ground to the throne of David, if the presumed father was of some other tribe or line. At the least it would have raised strong doubts in the Hebrew mind.

I realise that some may want to quote the case of Zelophehad's five daughters (Numbers 27), but it was exceptional and required a special law to make it legal and therefore provides only a limited special precedent. At this early stage Matthew wants to show that the mother of Jesus and his presumed father were both in the line of David, and therefore in the line of the Messiah.

It seems to me that Matthew is not just concerned with a precise legal argument but more to present a right conception. Let me give you an illustration of what I mean:

"So all the generations from Abraham to David are fourteen generations; and from David until the carrying away into Babylon are fourteen generations; and from the carrying away into Babylon unto Christ are fourteen generations."

(Matthew 1:17)

Notice that "from David until the carrying away into Babylon are *fourteen* generations". Now on the ground of strict accuracy that is not true. From David until the carrying away into Babylon is *eighteen* generations and Matthew has left out four names in this section. In verse 8 between Joram and Uzziah (or Ozias) there should be Ahaziah, Joash and Amaziah. Again in verse 11, between Josias and Jechoniah there should be Jehoiakim. Why did Matthew ignore these ancestors of the child of Mary? Probably because they had one common denominator – they were all men of consummate evil. Of the first three, Ahaziah, Joash and Amaziah were progeny of that daredevil pair Ahab and Jezebel. You will remember that at last there was virtually nothing left of Jezebel and it looks as though Matthew has so regarded her children – i.e., there is nothing to record and so he has ignored them.

When we come to Jehoiakim (verse 11), the verdict of Jeremiah speaks volumes. I quote from Jeremiah:

"Therefore thus saith the LORD concerning Jehoiakim the son of Josiah king of Judah; They shall not lament for him, saying, Ah my brother! or, Ah sister! they shall not lament for him, saying, Ah lord! or, Ah his glory! He shall be buried with the burial of an ass, drawn and cast forth beyond the gates of Jerusalem."   (22:18,19)

Do not these words make Jehoiakim non-existent in the eyes of God? It appears that in the eyes of Matthew he did not exist either.

So let us seek to understand it rightly: the genealogy is not a strict legal document, but the declaration of a right conception of the Messiah's forebears. Matthew is saying in effect: 'These are the only names which count in the genealogy of the Messiah – I have counted them and this is the account of his generations.'

Notice the three 'fourteen generation' cycles he proposes. The first begins with Abraham, the second with David and the third with the Babylonian captivity. In each case the inception of the cycle is significant and tells us something about Matthew's view of the Messiah. Abraham begins the first and he is the first man of the Hebrew race – the father of the elect. So in the mind of Matthew the Messiah is authenticated on the basis of race.

David, at the start of the second cycle, is pre-eminently the king of God's choosing – the man after God's own heart. So in the mind of Matthew the Messiah is authenticated on the principle of kingship – the Son of David, the anointed king.

Then the Babylonian captivity. It stands for the utter failure of the chosen race – Zion captured by Babylon. Zion, the synonym for obedience to the government of God issuing at last in peace, is mastered by Babylon, the synonym for rebellion against the government of God issuing at last in confusion. Into such a condition the Messiah came – the race enslaved, Zion mastered, and the people groping in darkness.

So in the mind of Matthew they wait for the liberator; they wait for the deliverer. They sigh for emancipation. The point is that at the end of his final cycle, Christ is related to the people's captivity. The cycle that began with enslavement ends with, "of whom was born Jesus who is called Christ". Into the captivity came Jesus, the anointed, the deliverer.

So out of the genealogy in the mind of Matthew, the child is authenticated as the Messiah on three counts: on the principle of race, on the principle of authority, and on the principle of his mission. Right at the beginning he is vindicated. This, it seems to me, is the real purpose of the genealogy.

"God with us"

Come now to Matthew's account of the child's birth:

> "Now all this was done, that it might be fulfilled which was spoken of the Lord by the prophet, saying, Behold, a virgin shall be with child, and shall bring forth a son, and they shall call his name Emmanuel, which being interpreted is, God with us. Then Joseph being raised from sleep did as the angel of the Lord had bidden him, and took unto him his wife."
>
> (Matthew 1:22-24)

It would be very nice to be able to spend a long time on the first fulfilment of these words in the days of Ahaz, as they were spoken by Isaiah (chapter 7), but we cannot do this. Sincere Bible students have differing views about who the child was in the first intention, and therefore who the virgin was. Some say the child was born to the wife of Isaiah (chapter 8) – the child with the difficult name: Maher-shalal-hash-baz. It means 'the spoil speedeth, the prey hasteth'. He was the sign to Ahaz that the enemies would be defeated but his own nation would be broken.

On the other hand there are those who believe the child was born to the young wife of Ahaz – his name was Hezekiah. He was also a man of sign. His mother's name was Abijah, which means 'Yah is Father'. If you want me to declare my preference, I go for Hezekiah as the virgin's child.

The use by the Holy Spirit of the Hebrew word *almah* for the mother is interesting. "A *virgin* shall conceive ..." The word *almah* means a young damsel of marriageable age, and therefore it would well describe the mother of Hezekiah, for she was very young, Ahaz being but eleven when his son was born. She was a virgin, she became pregnant and bore the child. But as you know the very same word in the mind of Matthew had an even more significant meaning – the virgin maid of Nazareth.

I do not think that when Isaiah says that he shall be called Immanuel he is making a theological declaration about the nature of the Messiah – such for instance as Paul is making in Colossians 2:9: "In him dwelleth all the fulness of the Godhead bodily." Paul's statement is telling us something very profound about the essential genesis of this man – the word "Godhead" is 'Deity'. 'In him dwelleth all the fulness of the Deity corporeally.' Isaiah is not on this level. By that I mean that I do not think we shall discover the meaning of Immanuel in the fullest sense in the text of the prophecy in Isaiah 7. It occurs twice in this part of the word of Isaiah and is not heard again until one day it falls from the lips of an angel for the sake of Joseph the carpenter of Nazareth.

The best illumination of Immanuel it seems to me is found in the words of Isaiah chapter 9. We have been with Ahaz and his enemies Rezin and Pekah, learning of his fear and desire for foreign aid. In chapter 9 the prophet is telling of tumult and tramping soldiers and garments fouled with blood, and then suddenly he is telling something quite different:

"For to us a child is born, to us a son is given; and the government will be upon his shoulder, and his name will be called 'Wonderful Counsellor, Mighty God, Everlasting Father, Prince of Peace.' Of the increase of his government and of peace there will be no end, upon the throne of David, and over his kingdom, to establish it, and to uphold it with justice and with righteousness from this time forth and for evermore. The zeal of the LORD of hosts will do this."

(Isaiah 9:6,7, RSV)

I put it to you honestly, is there a better more noble illumination of "God with us" than this? The spacious intention of the words in the mind of Matthew is discovered in the ancient word of Isaiah. Think of the four titles: "Wonderful Counsellor"; "Mighty God" or more accurately 'God Hero'; "Everlasting Father", or again more accurately 'Father of Eternity', and finally "Prince of Peace". I want to suggest to you that these four titles illuminate the meaning of "God with us" and at the same time they represent a process in the purpose of God: that is to say, the unveiling of God's activity in human experience – God with us.

The idea behind the title "Wonderful Counsellor" is that of creation. It relates to the one of perfect thought and perfect will – the one who makes all things good and without blemish, where there is never a mistake. The title "Wonderful Counsellor" expresses God's activity in creation.

Then "Mighty God" or 'God of Battles' – God who fights for His people and delivers them from their enemies.

Next "Everlasting Father" or 'Father of Eternity' – in the literal Hebrew, 'Father of the vanishing point': the one whose purpose extends beyond the limits of human time, the abiding one both as to time and space.

And finally "Prince of Peace", the one with revelation of peace and the authority to establish it. Here is the process – Creation, Salvation, Life and Peace. In other words, "God with us". The titles of the child are the revelation of God manifested among men; of God being near to humanity.

Of course God was ever near to those who shared humanity, in their pain and in their sorrow. In all their afflictions He was afflicted. But in the child, He was especially near to their consciousness. In a sense what was incomprehensible in Him became apprehendable. What once was inexplicable became visible, and Matthew as he unfolds his record will tell it.

He is the firstborn of the new creation which began with Him and in Him is fixed all the counsel and wisdom to establish it in the earth. He has the power to fight for His people and save them, and He will for He is *El Gibbor*, the "Mighty God", the 'God Hero'.

And then the ending of human time and human dominion, for then begins the eternity of which He is the begettor, leading to that peace which men desire but which they cannot secure, fixed only in Him who is the Prince.

So this, it seems to me, is the noblest meaning of Immanuel and it reveals superlatively the interpretation which Matthew inscribes upon the parchment of his Gospel – "God with us". It is telling us that God is not with us in order to sing a lullaby and soothe us with a narcotic. He is with us in order to establish judgement and justice and finally true peace. He is at war with all the forces which hurt and harm humanity. He is at war with all that is evil and diabolical. He cares for men in their awful predicament and in the child He cares for them superlatively. This is Immanuel and this is Matthew's Messiah.

"Call his name Jesus"
Our next step is to discover it even more poignantly in the name they gave to Mary's son as instructed by the angel:

> "But while [Joseph] thought on these things, behold, the angel of the Lord appeared unto him in a dream, saying, Joseph, thou son of David, fear not to take unto thee Mary thy wife: for that which is conceived in her is of the Holy Spirit. And she shall bring forth a son, and thou shalt call his name JESUS: for he shall save his people from their sins."
>
> (Matthew 1:20,21)

Those well tutored in the word of God will know that the name Jesus is the Greek form of the Hebrew name Joshua. If proof is needed it will be found in Hebrews 4:8. The Hebrew man is speaking of the fact that David prophesied about a future day of rest and then he adds: "For if Jesus had given them rest, then would he not afterward have spoken of another day." Obviously he is not referring to Jesus of Nazareth for he was not born in the days before David; he is speaking of Joshua the leader that followed Moses – and the Greek form of Joshua is Jesus. All other versions apart from the KJV in Hebrews 4:8 give Joshua as the name of the person referred to.

So let us mark it – Mary's son was called Joshua. I expect that Mary's friends and relatives would have shown no surprise that the boy was to be called Joshua nor would they ask what it meant. After all it was the name of the boy next door. It was a popular name among the Jews. It was the great hero name of the Hebrew people. Here is something to notice, that when God resolved to send His Son into the world as the Messiah, He chose a name ordinary, human, familiar, making him truly part of the human family. He chose a name that His people were using everywhere.

Remember how the name came into existence in Israel. The first man to bear it was Joshua the soldier. The name was given to him by Moses and the record is in Numbers 13:16. This man's name at first was Hoshea which means 'salvation'. Moses took it and interwove it with the name of God, Yahweh. Yahweh – Hoshea – Yahoshea – Yahshma – Joshua. It means 'Yah will save'. Subsequently many Hebrews bore the name but two received it with special distinction – Joshua the soldier and Joshua the high priest.

So it came to be the great hero name of the Hebrew nation. When the child was born he was named from heaven, and his name was registered by angels. Remember the angel's words: "Thou shalt call his name JESUS: for he shall save his people from their sins." Here is something to ponder – if only we knew the emphasis which the angel put upon the words. Which word did he stress? Was it *Jesus* or was it *people* or was it *sins*. The emphasis makes all the difference.

I believe we can form a good judgement helped by reading the Revised Version: "And she shall bring forth a son; and thou shalt call his name JESUS; for it is *he* that shall save his people from their sins." The emphasis is upon *he* – he it is that shall save his people. In other words, the emphasis upon *he* is making a contrast with the other Joshuas who have borne the name before. Joshua the soldier led the people into the land but on the admission of the Hebrew writer he could not give them rest. Joshua the high priest symbolically had the filthy garments taken away but it was only a symbol: the sins of the people remained. Joshua the high priest could not take away their sins. The two best Joshuas who ever lived could not save the people. They both failed. And then one day the child is born and he is named Joshua, because it is this Joshua who alone will fulfil the meaning of his name – 'Yah will save'. He is God's salvation.

All the promise of the past which ended in failure will be fulfilled with consummate success by this one lonely man, the Messiah. So one day he will stand among the people of Israel and say: "Come unto me, all ye that labour and are heavy laden, and I will give you rest." Matthew will tell us how he bore the shame of our disgrace and wore the filthy rags of our defilement even unto the shame of the cross, so that he might save his people from their sins and fulfil the destiny of his holy name. So the name Immanuel came to its noblest realisation in the fulfilling of the name of Jesus: the name that came to be above every name – Jesus, name of wondrous love.

Old Testament insight
In chapter 2 of Matthew's Gospel he makes four references to the Old Testament and each one in some way throws light upon his insight into the Messiah's high purpose. I wish there were time to look at them penetratingly but there is not. We shall have to be content with a very slender look at them. The first is from Micah and is in Matthew 2:6. It fixes the birthplace of the Messiah for

the Magi. I want you to notice how Matthew uses the word of
Micah. Look first at the words in Micah's prophecy:

"But thou, Bethlehem Ephratah, though thou be little among
the thousands of Judah, yet out of thee shall he come forth
unto me that is to be ruler in Israel; whose goings forth have
been from of old, from everlasting."   (Micah 5:2)

Now notice how Matthew quoted this – reading from the RV:

"And thou Bethlehem, land of Judah, art in no wise least
among the princes of Judah: for out of thee shall come forth
a governor, which shall be shepherd of my people Israel."

(Matthew 2:6)

The Holy Spirit using the mind of Matthew gives an insight into
the nature of the Messiah's mission: "which shall be shepherd of
my people Israel." Like his great progenitor he is to be a Shepherd
King. Isaiah had told us already (chapter 42): "Behold my servant
… mine elect in whom my soul delighteth" – he shall not break
the bruised reed or quench the smoking flax. Others will say, 'It
is bruised, it is no good'. He will say, 'It is only bruised, it can be
mended'. Others will say, 'It is smoking, put it out'. He will say,
'It is smoking, it can be fanned into flame'. The ruler will be a
shepherd. He will set judgement in the earth and carry the young
in his bosom – this is Matthew's Messiah.

Then verse 15, the quotation from Hosea 11:1: "Out of
Egypt have I called my son." Remember the words of Hosea: God
says, "When Israel was a child, then I loved him, and called my
son out of Egypt". So the deliverance from Egypt under Moses
was a manifestation of the love of God for His firstborn – the
people of Israel. He delivered them from the evil purposes of
a foreign king, the Pharaoh. Now once more the nation, in the
person of the child Messiah, is in Egypt as a result of the evil
purposes of a foreign king, Herod, the Idumean. So once more
He calls His Son out of Egypt to save the people. More than ever
it is a manifestation of the love of God. The child called out of
Egypt will one day build the city and lead the exodus and save
the people.

Then in Matthew chapter 2, we have the quotation from Jeremiah 31:15:

"In Rama was there a voice heard, lamentation, and weeping, and great mourning, Rachel weeping for her children, and would not be comforted, because they are not." (Matthew 2:18)

The strange thing about this quotation is that Jeremiah 31 is such a happy chapter, full of the joy of restoration, full of the promise of fulfilment. It is one of the great chapters we quote from to prove that God will gather His scattered nation and save them. But here is the mystery: right in the heart of it quite suddenly is the reference to Rachel weeping for her children and not willing to be comforted:

"Thus saith the LORD; A voice was heard in Ramah, lamentation, and bitter weeping; Rachel (RV) weeping for her children refused to be comforted for her children, because they were not." (Jeremiah 31:15)

Now let us notice carefully God's reply to this sadness:

"Thus saith the LORD; Refrain thy voice from weeping, and thine eyes from tears: for thy work shall be rewarded, saith the LORD; and they shall come again from the land of the enemy. And there is hope in thine end, saith the LORD, that thy children shall come again to their own border." (verses 16,17)

Now do you not think that when Matthew quoted this sad verse from Jeremiah 31 he would intend us to see the reply of God, that in the midst of the sorrow there is solace and hope for those bereaved and bereft? "Thy children shall come again." When Jesus was driven out there was weeping, and the inference is that when he returns there will be joy and salvation. Through the Messiah the tears will be dried and the children will sing again. The streets of Jerusalem will be full of boys and girls playing.

Then finally we come to verse 23 of Matthew 2: the prophets said that Jesus should be called a Nazarene. I must leave who said it and when. I shall accept Matthew's declaration unreservedly that it was said: he would be called a Nazarene, and so he was. There are different conclusions about its significance but I accept the conclusion that it is a term of reproach. Remember the saying, "Can any good thing come out of Nazareth?" Nazareth was a little town near the main highway but off the beaten track: near enough to know what was going on but not near enough to have any significance – a place bypassed. I am told that the word Nazareth comes from an old Hebrew word *netzer* which means a sprout or branch. Nazareth was like a sprout sticking out of the earth – a place on a hill. It was just a sprout having nothing to commend it. The tree is gone, only a sprout is left.

Now here is something to ponder – the word *netzer* which is thought to be the origin of Nazareth, is the very word used in Isaiah to describe the Messiah. Remember: "And there shall come forth a shoot out of the stock of Jesse, and a branch out of his roots shall bear fruit" (Isaiah 11:1, RV). The Hebrew word rendered "branch" is *netzer*. I say it is a term of despising, referring to a man from a place of no consequence. He was despised and rejected of men: a Nazarene. But Matthew will show us before long that the Nazarene of men is in the sight of God the Exalted One. He is exiled and hated but soon he will be received and glorified. The little sprout will come as the Branch in flaming advent glory. The Nazarene is crowned with many crowns.

So there it is. From the four Old Testament references Matthew gives us a vision of the Messiah. He is to be a Shepherd King – strong and gentle. His enemies shall lick the dust but he shall lead his flock into green pastures. He will deliver his people from bondage – he will bring them out of Egypt and destroy their enemies. He will turn weeping into joy: Rachel will sing and the children will dance. The despised one will be given dominion – He is King and High Priest.

This is Matthew's Messiah.

The first message and the manifesto

Matthew 3 and 4

W HEN we say 'the first message' we mean first chronologically, but also first in importance – as before long we hope to prove. But to begin with let us notice Matthew's method:

"In those days came John the Baptist, preaching in the wilderness of Judaea ..."   (3:1)

"Then cometh Jesus from Galilee to Jordan unto John ..."
(verse 13)

First came John preaching, then after that came Jesus. It would be sensible to follow this pattern. If we are to understand better the coming of the Messiah into public life, let us look briefly at the coming of his forerunner – because this is what Matthew does.

The ministry of John the Baptist

Notice the message of John: "Repent ye: for the kingdom of heaven is at hand" (verse 2), and then: "Bring forth therefore fruits meet for repentance" (verse 8). John is a realist. He had learned in the desert that reality lies at the root of all religious life. To a nation of formalists he came preaching that they must be real. *Personal* reformation is required in preparation for the kingdom of heaven.

From Luke's record we learn just how practical his message was. Let each man do his duty. Let the rich give to those who are poor. Let the publican accuse no man falsely. Let the soldier be content with his wages. Change yourselves or you will have no kingdom at all. He delivered his message manfully and his success was astonishing, even to himself. He was a burning and a shining light and he burned his way into the hearts of the Israelites as the desert swarmed with crowds.

The formalist was not satisfied any longer with his formalism and the unbeliever could not rest any longer on his infidelity. They said, 'What must we do?' The answer – comfort the bereft and feed the starving. Let us mark the message carefully. Though he was a hermit John took no half view of men and things. There was nothing morbid in his call to the nation. "Repent", with him did not mean, 'Come with me into the wilderness and live away from the world'. No – it meant, 'Go back to the world and live above it', each doing his worldly duty in an unworldly spirit. The result was a strange thing. Men of the world, hard men and cynical men, came with reverence to learn the true duties of an active life in a busy bustling world from a man who lived all his life in the desert.

What was the secret of John's success, this voice crying in the wilderness? As it appears to me, one strong reason was that men felt John was real. They knew they could not go to him, as they could to the rabbis, for some learned subtlety, some piece of sophistry. His words were real and touched them powerfully: 'Repent – wrath is to come – the axe is laid at the root – fruitless trees will be cast into the fire.' He preached as men preach when they are in earnest. They may not have liked it but they could not escape its realism. So they felt, I think, that John was true. He had the power of confronting each man's life with the awful truth about its shallowness.

So the poor look wistfully for some solace and salvation; the soldiers reverence John's heroism; the guilty publicans come for purification of heart; the self-satisfied formalist is ready to confess his shallowness, and the calm reasoning infidel comes to shed his scepticism. Remember John's reaction to these latter two classes: "Who hath warned you to flee from the wrath to come?" Even John marvelled that such as these had responded. Perhaps all this empty show has no real conviction after all.

Formalism can never satisfy truly the man who is seeking God, nor will scepticism give any true rest to the troubled spirit.

The formalist's heart is perhaps polluted and miserable, and the infidel who is so sure and certain, perhaps after all is restless and dark and desolate. Why do I say it? Well ask yourself, 'Why are these men trembling on the brink of Jordan?' Perhaps inferentially they are telling us something as they wait upon the bank of John's river: 'It is a lie, we are not happy, we are dark and hopeless and miserable.'

Matthew finds his Hebrew justification for the mission of John the herald in the great fortieth chapter of Isaiah:

"Comfort ye, comfort ye my people, saith your God. Speak ye comfortably to Jerusalem, and cry unto her, that her warfare is accomplished, that her iniquity is pardoned: for she hath received of the LORD's hand double for all her sins. The voice of him that crieth in the wilderness, Prepare ye the way of the LORD, make straight in the desert a highway for our God. Every valley shall be exalted, and every mountain and hill shall be made low: and the crooked shall be made straight, and the rough places plain: and the glory of the LORD shall be revealed, and all flesh shall see it together: for the mouth of the LORD hath spoken it."   (Isaiah 40:1-5)

The implication is incisive. The one whom Isaiah describes is about to appear. By the mystery of the Spirit, Isaiah had heard the voice of John crying in the wilderness – but very soon Isaiah will move from the herald to the herald's king: "Behold my servant ... mine elect, in whom my soul delighteth ... He shall not fail nor be discouraged, till he have set judgement in the earth" (Isaiah 42:1-4).

Isaiah tells us what the outcome will be: "Every valley shall be exalted, and every mountain and hill shall be made low: and the crooked shall be made straight, and the rough places plain: and the glory of the LORD shall be revealed, and all flesh shall see it together." The kingdom of the heavens is at hand. Surely Matthew meant us to understand this when he hovered over the prophet's reference to the voice in the wilderness.

Finally notice how Matthew tells us what the coming one was to be like through the selected words of John the herald. He will destroy and he will build, this Messiah. He will break and he will heal. John says he will cleanse the threshing-floor. He is a man with a fan and with unquenchable fire. The axe is ready and the workman is strong. The fan winnows and the fire will purify. Notice the blessing: he shall gather his wheat into the garner. We can let our imagination interpret the testimony of John. The Messiah will not make a truce with the things in any man's life which are in opposition to the purity of God. Matthew in his tenth chapter records that the Man of Nazareth said: "I came not to bring peace, but a sword." He will not come and then temporise with evil. He is at war with the forces which contradict the divine ideal of peace – in the soul and in the world. He is at war with pride and greed and inflated self-importance. As you hear the word of John about the Messiah – that he will throughly purge the threshing-floor – know this, that he is at war with the forces which thrive upon fear. He is at war with the jackboot and the torturers. He is at war with the forces which starve and rob and murder. Let us thank God that his enemies shall lick the dust; thank God also that he is a garnering Messiah. Isaiah says of Yahweh's servant, the anointed one:

"I the LORD have called thee in righteousness, and will hold thine hand, and will keep thee, and give thee for a covenant of the people, for a light of the Gentiles; to open the blind eyes, to bring out the prisoners from the prison, and them that sit in darkness out of the prison house."   (Isaiah 42:6,7)

Finally mark one thing John says about the Messiah: "He that cometh after me is mightier than I, whose shoes I am not worthy to bear." What a splendid epilogue to the testimony of John about the anointed one. Jesus said John was the greatest born of women; John says he was not worthy to undo the latchet of Jesus' shoe. No wonder it is recorded: "Let all the angels of God worship him." Notice the first word in verse 13 of chapter 3: "Then cometh Jesus from Galilee ..." "Then" means 'at that time', that particular time when John had cried and stirred the nation and prepared the way – when John had done his work, "*then* cometh Jesus from Galilee".

The baptism of Jesus

We cannot dwell for very long upon the baptism of Jesus, but we cannot pass it by. The main question to interest us is, 'Why did it happen?' Measured by human judgement it is a contradiction. The baptism of John was a baptism of repentance and Jesus was sinless. Rude people might say it was just a performance – an empty show. There he was, the Messiah, the sinless one among the sinful, the prince of life among the dead, submitting to baptism as a sign of repentance. Even John was surprised: John left to himself would have said 'No'. The justification is focused in the word of Jesus: "Suffer it to be so now: for thus it becometh us to fulfil all righteousness."

There is no need to beat about the bush. It appears to me this is why it happened – this is what Jesus meant by fulfilling all righteousness. Yes he was sinless and had no need of repentance, not one whit. Notwithstanding, he did it to identify himself with those who are sin-stricken and in need of redemption. It was an act to associate himself with his great mission. If the Messiah was intended to be just an exemplar, an example of a good life, then the baptism would have been pointless. But he is not just an example, he is a redeemer. The redeemer is identified with the redeemed; the sinless with the sinful. There is a sentence in Isaiah 53 which may illuminate it: "He was numbered with the transgressors." I know we usually think of that as referring to his death, but may not the baptism have been a beginning of the process – a prophecy of the final baptism, the baptism of blood? So he identifies himself with the people he is to save and over whom eventually he is to reign. Paul says, "he humbled himself, and became obedient unto death". Is not his baptism a sign of death? Later on he will say: "I have a baptism to be baptized with; and how am I straitened till it be accomplished!" So in view of the world at his baptism he consecrated himself to that righteousness which will end with the cross.

John says: "Behold the Lamb of God, which taketh away the sin of the world." A man cannot gather and garner until he gives himself away. He who loses his life shall find it. He renounces in his immersion the sin he has renounced all his life. That the baptism of Jesus was right there can be no doubt and two things prove it. The Holy Spirit descends in rich effusion – the power and light of heaven flood into his soul. And then the voice of God. If you listen carefully you can hear the note of contentment in the voice from heaven. The God who rested after His great creative week was soon disturbed by the rebellion of man, and was rising early and sending His prophets. But now there is contentment in heaven. "This is my beloved Son, in whom I am well pleased." His years of dedicated life at Nazareth have won the divine approbation.

Mark the words carefully. The Father was "well pleased". It means the carpenter is anointed to be the Lord's Christ. The other thing to notice is the dove. Matthew is revealing the Messiah to the Hebrews and there were two things that in the Hebrew mind stood markedly for sacrifice: the lamb and the dove. In the baptism he had consented to death for the saving of men from their sin. The dove was the sacrifice for sin offered by the poorest and the humblest. These were not idle things: they tell and foretell the deep things of his high calling.

Listen to this: "Christ ... through the eternal Spirit offered himself without blemish unto God" (Hebrews 9:14, RV). We can begin to understand the Psalmist: "Yet have I set my king upon my holy hill of Zion" (Psalm 2:6). God is content.

Dwelling in Capernaum

Come now to Matthew chapter 4:

"Now when Jesus had heard that John was cast into prison, he departed into Galilee; and leaving Nazareth, he came and dwelt in Capernaum, which is upon the sea coast, in the borders of Zabulon and Nephthalim: that it might be fulfilled which was spoken by Esaias the prophet, saying, The land of Zabulon, and the land of Nephthalim, by the way of the sea, beyond Jordan, Galilee of the Gentiles; the people which sat in darkness saw great light; and to them which sat in the region and shadow of death light is sprung up."

(Matthew 4:12-16)

What an interesting thing. Jesus had lived at Nazareth for thirty years but suddenly he left there altogether and took up residence in Capernaum. He did this when John was imprisoned. Once again Matthew takes us to the Old Testament by way of explanation. He says the action was in fulfilment of Isaiah the prophet. The passage quoted is right at the start of that chapter we have already pondered where the child is celebrated in the four couplets, Wonderful Counsellor, Mighty God, Everlasting Father, and Prince of Peace:

"Nevertheless the dimness shall not be such as was in her vexation, when at the first he lightly afflicted the land of Zebulun and the land of Naphtali, and afterward did more grievously afflict her by the way of the sea, beyond Jordan, in Galilee of the nations [Gentiles]. The people that walked in darkness have seen a great light: they that dwell in the land of the shadow of death, upon them hath the light shined."

(Isaiah 9:1,2)

I am told by those who understand these things better than I do, that the land of Zebulon and Naphtali was the land that suffered most of all from the invasion of the Assyrians and which was regarded as being the most degraded part of all Israel because of its contamination from Gentile influence and Gentile presence. So you will notice it is called "Galilee of the Gentiles" – in a sense, a term of disgust. I have read that because of this degradation, it was actually known by the Jews as, "The region and shadow of death". In the heart of it was Capernaum by the seaside. It came to be known as his own city. Here Jesus found the man who wrote this Gospel. The point is that here at Capernaum he went deliberately to the worst place – the place of the deepest darkness – the lowest place, literally and spiritually, so they said; the despised place, the place of degradation, the place where the people walk in darkness. And there the great light shone forth.

The wonder is that Isaiah had seen it: "To them which sat in the region and shadow of death light is sprung up." This is where the message was proclaimed. Notice what it was: "From that time began Jesus to preach, and to say, Repent: for the kingdom of heaven is at hand" (Matthew 4:17). The words are familiar. We heard them first from the lips of John the Baptist: the very same message from John and Jesus.

I am going now to say what might be regarded as controversial; that is to say, you may disagree with it strongly. Although the cry was the same, there is a difference between the message of John and the message of Jesus. This is what I mean. John said, 'Repent and prepare yourselves for the way of the Lord – change your conduct, stop your dishonesty, your greed, your exclusivism'. He put his finger on their wickedness and said, 'Stop it – change your doings'. The King came and said, 'Repent' – and he meant also change your conduct, but it was deeper and more incisive. He faced men squarely and said that they were wrong not only in their conduct but in their consciousness. They were wrong in their thinking, in their minds, in the centre of things – 'Get right there', was his message. This was utterly radical, it was a revolution. It is fundamental and essential. A man's consciousness regulates his conduct and his conduct formulates his character. As a man "thinketh in his heart, so is he" (Proverbs 23:7). Notice the implication. You cannot change the centre by tinkering with the circumference. A man's heart is not changed by renovating the externalities. How you are in your consciousness conditions how you behave, and how you behave makes you what you are in your character. Put it to the test. If you believe truly in the kingdom of God you will know that this life is not the real life for the disciples of the King; that their real vocation begins in the age to come, and that now they are but pilgrims going onward to their true destiny and to their true life. If you believe that, it will condition your attitude to the present life. If you really believe you are a pilgrim you will not be obsessed with the pursuit of pleasure, with the gaining of worldly wisdom, with the acquisition of things. Because here you are only on probation you will handle with light hands the things of this life, be it rank, status, pleasure, or possessions. This happens because of what you believe about the kingdom of God. Other men will say you are mad, but you know that it is a madness which really is the sublimest sanity. That is what I mean then – what you believe in your deepest heart is vital. This I believe was the message of the King.

"The kingdom of heaven is at hand"
The word "repent" from his lips passes into the deepest things of a man's fundamental faith. It means get right at the centre. When shortly we come to look at his manifesto, we shall find this is confirmed. But for now mark his reason for the repentance: "The kingdom of heaven is at hand." With our sure belief in the future kingdom of God on earth, we need a moment to explain the meaning of that proclamation made two thousand years ago: "The kingdom of *heaven* is *at hand*." The kingdom of heaven is the Hebrew way of referring to the rule of heaven upon earth – that is to say, the kingdom of God. It occurs mostly in the Gospel of Matthew because he was writing especially for the Hebrew nation. It is not the kingdom of earth – that would be a travesty of its meaning. It is on earth but it is the rule of heaven; the rule of the Most High over the affairs of men. Now Jesus said that because of the kingdom of heaven, men should change their minds and their conduct and their character. They must now enthrone God in their lives, bow the knee at His throne, kiss the sceptre of His rule, swear their allegiance to His government. For the sake of any who are not sure, it means the rule of the King upon earth administering the sovereignty of God over all people – the kingdom of God.

The prophets had all testified to the abiding fact of this kingdom, that one day it would be established upon earth and it would never be destroyed. Men sing in hope and they wail in agony and they cry in despair, and what they need is the coming of the King to establish the government of God in the world. This is what is meant by the words "the kingdom of heaven". Jesus made it plain in the pattern prayer, "Thy will be done in earth, as it is in heaven". All heaven is to be let loose on earth.

But here is the mystery: Jesus said it was "*at hand*". Let us not beat about the bush – it was at hand because the King himself was in their midst. That is what he meant once by "the kingdom of God is within you" (Luke 17:21). That is a very bad translation; what he said was, "the kingdom of God is in the midst of you". What he meant was, 'Accept me as King and you have come close to citizenship; obey me and eventually the doors of the kingdom will be opened to you. Submit to my commands and you have grasped the very values of my kingdom'. It is by the way of the King that men will come at last to the kingdom.

This is how the prophets saw it. They looked with wistful eyes from the mountain tops and told of the coming of a child, a Son, and the government was to be upon his shoulder. Wonderful Counsellor, Mighty God, Everlasting Father, Prince of Peace: this was the child in his maturity. And the result?

"Of the increase of his government and peace there shall be no end, upon the throne of David, and upon his kingdom, to order it, and to establish it with judgement and with justice from henceforth even for ever. The zeal of the LORD of hosts will perform this." (Isaiah 9:7)

Those who came to understand this knew that when the King stood among the people of God the kingdom of heaven was at hand.

The Sermon on the Mount

We move on to Matthew chapter 5:

"And seeing the multitudes, he went up into the mountain: and when he was set, his disciples came unto him: and he opened his mouth, and taught them."

We call it the manifesto – sometimes called the Sermon on the Mount. Have you ever met the people who say to us, 'We do not care for your Statement of Faith, for your strong doctrinal attitude, for your defined dogmas, for your formulated tenets – we do not like this; all we want is the Sermon on the Mount'. It's as though they say: 'Your doctrine is complicated, controversial and difficult, but give us the Sermon on the Mount – that is straightforward, clear, and without dispute. All we want is the Sermon on the Mount.' Does that make you smile?

Is there anything more difficult than the Sermon on the Mount? Is there anything more likely to turn you inside out than the Sermon on the Mount? Is there a more radical declaration in the Bible than the Sermon on the Mount? All we want is the Sermon on the Mount! I would have thought that if we are looking for quietness and non-complication and easy living without being disturbed, the very last thing we want is the Sermon on the Mount. Remember its demands:

- When you are reproached and persecuted and vilified, rejoice and be exceeding glad.
- Everyone that looks on a woman to lust after her has committed adultery in his heart.
- If your right eye causes you to stumble, pluck it out, and if your right hand causes you to stumble cut it off.
- Resist not evil, but whosoever smites you on your right cheek, turn to him the other also.
- If any man takes your coat, give him your cloke also.
- Whosoever compels you to go a mile, go with him two.
- Give to him that asks you, and from him that would borrow of you, turn not away.
- Love your enemies and pray for them that despitefully use you.
- Judge not, that you be not judged, for with what judgement you judge, you shall be judged.
- You shall be perfect, as your heavenly Father is perfect.

All we want is the Sermon on the Mount? If you want revolution, here it is. The King says that the blessed people are those who are poor, who mourn, who are meek, who hunger and thirst, who are merciful, who are pure in heart, peacemakers and are persecuted. All we want is the Sermon on the Mount? This is radical and outrageous. It is the King's manifesto and measured by human measurement is the recipe for failure.

Why is it so radical, so heart-searching, so scorching? Because of something we have marked already – it seeks to touch men at the centre of things. It searches the internal; it changes the heart. Never mind adultery in some dark place, done furtively in secret – what about adultery committed in the heart, and in the mind? Does that make you shudder? Have you ever said quietly to yourself, 'Would it not be better if the standard were a little lower?' Think of this again: "Be ye therefore perfect, even as your Father which is in heaven is perfect" (Matthew 5:48). In the compass of perfection is there not that which could be called the middle range?

Hear the voice of the King to a lawyer: "Thou shalt love the Lord thy God with all thy heart, and with all thy soul, and with all thy mind. This is the great and first commandment." Is that what he said? No, it is not. This is what he said: "Thou shalt love the Lord thy God with thy *whole* heart, and with thy *whole* soul, and with thy *whole* mind." There is a word for "all" and there is a word for "whole", and he said, "whole". You think I am splitting hairs? Come to Malachi. God says: "Bring ye all the tithes into the storehouse ... and prove me now herewith, saith the LORD of hosts, if I will not open you the windows of heaven ..." (Malachi 3:10). Hear it in the RV: "Bring ye the *whole* tithe into the storehouse". What is the difference between "all" and the "whole"? "All" is the sum total of the tithes together, neatly added up and presented – externally correct. The "whole" tithe is the sum total of the tithes added up – and in addition the spirit in which they are brought. Because the spirit is an essential part of the offering, the right spirit turns "all" into the "whole". "All" is quantitative; the "whole" is qualitative. That is why the manifesto is so radical. That is why the ethic of Jesus is so revolutionary. The Messiah urges perfection because without it a man may do the very thing which Jesus commands and yet still not have the spirit of the one who commands it.

Seeking perfection takes us into the realm of the inward, the real, the spirit. To have lowered the standard would have been to miss the whole purpose of the ethic. So when the King pronounces his blessings right at the beginning of the manifesto, notice that no blessing is pronounced upon anyone for having anything or doing anything, but instead every blessing is pronounced upon men for what they are inwardly. That is not to deny that there are external actions and attitudes which of necessity reveal the fact of righteousness, but if the heart is wrong, there is no beatitude. "Blessed are the pure in heart, for they shall see God."

So this is the revelation of Matthew's Messiah according to the manifesto. It is not the overt act of sin which is supremely to be condemned, but rather the inner lust which seeks after the sin. It tells us that God does not shudder as men shudder. Men shudder at the outward sign of sin – the murderer with blood on his hands, the adulterer caught in the act. But God shudders most at those things in a man's soul – contempt, hatred, envy, lust, which presently will express themselves in overt sin, and which often are restrained only by lack of opportunity. This is why the manifesto urges perfection, because without it the very deepest things of a man's nature would not be touched. Give men the attainable and they will soon be satisfied; perhaps even boastful men are wooed and won by the ideal. The second best, the compromised, the counterfeit will never do that. It is the call of the ideal and the vision of perfection which drive a man to strive.

So the great light of the King's manifesto flashes upon his disciples – searching, revealing, shaming – sometimes blinding them with its intensity. Let us not be dismayed. The Messiah will take the central essential fact of human personality – the mind – and link it with the word of God, making our senses keen for the knowledge of His purpose, step by step transforming the desires of the heart and of the mind. Perfection is the ideal, but for those who fall short, there is mercy and compassion. Remember he takes us as we are, with the pollution upon us, and makes us at last to be like himself.

Let us thank God for the loving mercy of Matthew's Messiah.

3 |

The King and his kingdom
Matthew 21:33-46

N OBODY can take up this Gospel of Matthew reverently and read it with an open mind and honest heart and not be compelled to say that it presents to us a personality utterly unique and supremely wonderful. I know there are those who say that the Messiah never existed – that he was imagined by people with fanciful minds who created somebody they wanted to meet and follow, but really it was all in their lively minds. A great hoax – a brilliant fantasy. Well, if they are right, all I can say is that I would very much have liked to meet the men who imagined him, for they must have been the most accomplished and marvellous people the world has ever seen. To be able to create an imaginary character who has turned the world upside down and affected almost every avenue of human endeavour and human activity, they must have been greater than Shakespeare, than Plato, than Homer.

There is no doubt, the great revelation of Matthew about this man is that he is the King. He is also a lawgiver, he is a physician, but pre-eminently he is the King. He is a masterpiece. His words are the simplest and yet they are the sublimest. He repels people with his severity and woos them with his compassion. He baffles all attempts to understand him purely on the human level.

"My beloved Son, in whom I am well pleased"
There is about him a mystery. I want to bring you back to something in the Gospel of Matthew which we have looked at already lightly, but which we ought to look at again a little more

penetratingly. It is the voice from heaven which said: "This is my beloved Son, in whom I am well pleased" (3:17). This is the explanation of the mystery. We may never understand it fully this side of the kingdom of God, but these words account for the uniqueness of the man. What I mean is that the declaration from heaven is confirmed as true by observing the things he said, the life he lived, and the work he accomplished.

For example, would you not agree that this declaration explains the kingly authority of this lonely man? Once they sent officers to arrest him, and they came back without him and when they were asked why they had not brought him the soldiers' explanation was this: "Never man spake like this man." Ponder it – is there anything in the Gospel narrative more extraordinary? Armed soldiers sent to arrest one unarmed teacher and they dare not or could not because of the words he spoke. They could not challenge his authority. If you accept that there is laughter in heaven I can well believe that the angels laughed as they watched the soldiers being arrested by the man they were sent to arrest. So when we hear the voice from heaven, "This is my Son, the beloved", what do we think of? Where does our memory rest? Well, it seems to me that we would be thinking of Psalm 2: "The LORD hath said unto me, Thou art my Son; this day have I begotten thee." What we have to remember is that when this voice came from heaven, in a sense it was breaking the silence of some four hundred years. It is therefore a moment of great solemnity in the history of the chosen people.

It is the first recorded word of God the Father about the child. In a way it is a strange merging of the eternal and the temporal. "This is my beloved Son": the Son who had been intended from the beginning in the purpose of God – this is eternal. Then, "in thee I am well pleased". This is the comment of heaven upon the life lived at Nazareth – this is the temporal. What we must do is to take the words of Matthew and look at them in the light of the words of the second Psalm:

"Yet have I set my King upon my holy hill of Zion. I will declare the decree: the LORD hath said unto me, Thou art my *Son*; this day have I begotten thee ... Kiss the *Son*, lest he be angry, and ye perish from the way, when his wrath is kindled but a little. Blessed are all they that put their trust in him."

(Psalm 2:6,7,12)

The word "Son" in the first quotation, "Thou art my *Son*" is not the same as the word "Son" in verse 12 – "Kiss the *Son*, lest he be angry ..." The first "Son" is the Hebrew word *ben*; the second is the Hebrew (borrowed from the Aramaic) word *bar*. There is a distinction to be drawn between these two words which could be significant. They occur in Hebrew names – hence we have Ben-jamin, Ben-Hur; we have Bartimaeus Bar-Jonah. Now the difference is this. The word *ben* has to do with the one who builds the house and continues the race or the line. It is a peculiarly Hebrew idea – the responsibility for the solidarity of the family line. So *ben* has in it the idea of Son of the right hand, the builder of the house, the continuer of the genealogy of the history. I have read that old Hebrews when asked how old they are, in reply sometimes give the age of the family – say 1,000 years. This is the concept behind the word *ben*.

On the other hand the word *bar* relates to inheritance. *Bar* means the heir. So the first word declares the responsibility and the second indicates the blessing. In the Psalm both words are used of the Son. First of all as to nature: 'Thou art my Son, the son of the right hand, the continuer of the house, the begetter of the race, the anointed'. Then as to inheritance, the Son is the heir of God; he will share all the wealth of the divine purpose.

So *ben* – "Thou art my Son, this day have I begotten thee"; and *bar* – "Ask of me, and I shall give thee the heathen [nations] for thine inheritance, and the uttermost parts of the earth for thy possession". The Messiah is God's Son in the truest sense and at the same time His heir, realising His great purpose and ruling the world with justice and with mercy. "Kiss the Son, lest he be angry, and ye perish from the way", for his wrath will soon be kindled. "Blessed are all they that put their trust in him."

So this is what I mean by the merging of the eternal and the temporal. The Son – the eternal, in the mind of John, the

Logos, the Hebrew wisdom, the one who had glory with the Father before the world was; the one slain from the foundation of the world; the one who before Abraham was the "I am"; the *phanerosis* of God. And then, "In thee I am well pleased".

We know hardly anything about the life of the Son during the years at Nazareth after his visit to the temple. Briefly the veil was lifted there when he said: "Wist ye not that I must be about my Father's business?" Evidently he had some mysterious insight as to who he was and what he had to do. We do not know how he had lived, but we know that it pleased God: a man on earth conforming utterly to the heavenly pattern; the temporal perfectly in harmony with the eternal; a human Christ allowing nothing to master him but the will of his Father; the pure in the midst of the impure; the perfect one bending to the lowliness of the carpenter's shop. No wonder the voice said, "I am well pleased". This is vital because right at the outset of the account of Matthew's Messiah we have the divine approval upon this revelation of the King.

Why it is so important is this. I ask you a question. Can you give your allegiance, your final and absolute allegiance to some earthly King who is fallible and weak and selfish? Is it not true that no man or woman conscious of their manhood or womanhood can commit the whole mastery of their being to some other man without question? Or put in another way – no mere man can exercise final authority over other men. The only complete and final authority which can be accepted for the dignity of human life is the authority of God. In the end there can be no other King but God.

The Gospel of the kingdom

So you see, it is essential that the voice speaks from heaven. How else can we be sure that he is the anointed, the one to whom we can submit in perfect confidence. If God is satisfied, we have no cause for doubt. "Yet have I set my King upon my holy hill of Zion." If he is King in the thought of God, how can we demur? Do you agree with God about this Man of Nazareth? Just for a moment I venture, I hope with your approval, into the Gospel

of John and read about an Israelite who looked into the face of
Jesus and said: "Rabbi, thou art the Son of God; thou art the King
of Israel" (John 1:49). There is Psalm 2 and Matthew 3 – a man
who agreed with God. The man of the seamless robe, who has
nowhere to lay his head – he is God's King.

Let us look at it from another level. Think of conditions
eighty years ago. There were plenty of some things and there was
a shortage of others. There was plenty of destitution; there was a
shortage of affluence. They were hard times: no pension, no dole;
if you were out of work you were very hard pressed indeed – there
was virtually nothing. If you had work, the hours were long and
the wages low. One sister told me she worked from 8 am to 8 pm
as a shop assistant and up to 9 pm on Saturdays, leaving at 11 pm
after things were checked and righted for Monday morning. The
ecclesia in Oxford used to pay a brother six-pence per week to
light and dowse the candles in our meeting room – it helped to
feed his children. The ecclesia bought a second-hand mangle for
a widow so that she could take in washing and keep alive.

In those days scarlet fever was a notifiable disease and
victims were segregated. A brother and sister's children caught
it and the husband could not go to work for over six weeks: no
work, no money. The day came when the mother handed the
baker her last coin and said, 'You need not call again, that is the
last of our money'. Let it be put on record that the baker was a
good man. He said, 'While I have bread, you will have bread'. And
so it came to pass. If you are wondering how they came to be so
bereft – a family of the ecclesia – I am wondering too, but we shall
never know and it is best to leave it. In the ecclesial minutes the
Recording Brother has written: "Today there were three buttons
in the collection bag", and added wryly, "It is hoped that this
practice will not continue". When people have only buttons to
give they are very poor. All this I say to remind you of the times
– they were hard and without much hope.

Now into this society there came the Gospel of the kingdom
of God. Beset by the hardness of life it was like a bolt from the blue,
a shaft of light in a dark world, a song in the long night. It came to

be their master comfort. Those who dream dreams and see visions, they believed in it and they loved it. It was sweetness being poured into the rancid stream of life. It was saffron being cast upon the dullness of the day. It promised joy for sadness. Their sorrow was succoured and there was healing for their wounds. They longed for the coming of the Son of God. They never ceased to talk of it. The idea of wanting to postpone it would be to them the supreme contradiction. It was the one thing they wanted above all other because it answered their need superlatively. You can imagine how they brooded over visions of the kingdom like Isaiah 11:

> "And there shall come forth a rod out of the stem of Jesse, and a Branch shall grow out of his roots: and the spirit of the LORD shall rest upon him, the spirit of wisdom and understanding, the spirit of counsel and might, the spirit of knowledge and of the fear of the LORD; and shall make him of quick understanding in the fear of the LORD: and he shall not judge after the sight of his eyes, neither reprove after the hearing of his ears: but with righteousness shall he judge the poor, and reprove with equity for the meek of the earth: and he shall smite the earth with the rod of his mouth, and with the breath of his lips shall he slay the wicked. And righteousness shall be the girdle of his loins, and faithfulness the girdle of his reins. The wolf also shall dwell with the lamb, and the leopard shall lie down with the kid; and the calf and the young lion and the fatling together; and a little child shall lead them. And the cow and the bear shall feed; their young ones shall lie down together: and the lion shall eat straw like the ox. And the sucking child shall play on the hole of the asp, and the weaned child shall put his hand on the cockatrice' den. They shall not hurt nor destroy in all my holy mountain: for the earth shall be full of the knowledge of the LORD, as the waters cover the sea."   (Isaiah 11:1-9)

Many a weary head rested upon those words of comfort. Many a broken spirit found healing there. Many a fearful and frightened soul took courage through those promises.

Those words had a profound effect upon the people seventy to eighty years ago because they are profound words. No

wonder they loved the vision so dearly and saw it so clearly. What
we do occasionally, they did regularly – dwell longingly upon the
blessings of the kingdom of God. To them these things were
rousing, invigorating, exciting. Now the thing I want to stress is
this. The thing that stirred their hearts and gave them new hope
was not the teaching that the kingdom of God was the rule of
Christ in the hearts of men. That they had heard before. Nor was
it the teaching that the kingdom of God was the church, nor was
it that the hope of the righteous was to go to heaven at death
and dwell in bliss and felicity. They were not roused and excited
by some misty phantasmagoria of demons, devils and angels. Let
us not mistake it one whit. The thing that filled their hearts with
new joy and lit their face with new hope was the Gospel of the
kingdom of God on earth at the appearing of the Great King and
Saviour in flaming advent glory.

I say all this to stress that according to Matthew this was the
Gospel of the kingdom of God which the Messiah preached amid
the streets and hills of Galilee, in the synagogues of Judaea and
in the metropolitan life of Jerusalem. He preached the Gospel of
the kingdom of God (Matthew 4:23). In the Gospel of Matthew,
the anointed King is revealed as the Son of David eventually to
sit on David's throne, and rule over the house of Jacob. James
and John wanted to sit with Christ on his throne in positions
of authority. The dying thief asked for remembrance when the
Christ came in his kingdom. Some will see Abraham, Isaac and
Jacob sitting down in that kingdom and they themselves cast
out. Jesus will not drink of the fruit of the vine until he drinks
it new with his disciples in the kingdom. When his disciples ask
him about the restoration of the kingdom to Israel, he does not
rebuke them for their foolishness but says they must leave God to
work out His own calendar. For forty days after his resurrection
he spoke to them of the things pertaining to the kingdom of God.
It was after that long session about the kingdom that they asked:
"Wilt thou at this time restore again the kingdom to Israel?"

In Matthew's Gospel, Jesus is called "King of the Jews";
in Revelation 1, the "King of the earth"; in John 12, the "King

of Israel"; in Hebrews 8, the "King of Salem"; in Revelation 17 and 19, the "King of kings". One day he will sit upon the throne of his glory and say to some, "Come, ye blessed of my Father, inherit the kingdom prepared for you from the foundation of the world" (Matthew 25:34).

If you saying in bewilderment, why is he telling us all this? It is because I am weary of people who want to convince us that the kingdom preached by Jesus was in some way different from that preached by the prophets; that they thought of it on a low material level and Jesus came and taught us it was something spiritual and ethical and far superior to the physical kingdom of Isaiah and Daniel. In Matthew 21 there is the record of how the Man of Nazareth entered Jerusalem triumphantly on a colt and an ass. A very great multitude spread their garments in his way and others cut down branches from the trees and strewed them in his path. And they cried, "Hosanna to the son of David: Blessed is he that cometh in the name of the Lord; Hosanna in the highest".

The word "Hosanna" means 'save us', or 'save us now'. This was deliberately planned and executed by Jesus and it seems evident that it was intended to be an official claim to the kingship of Israel. This is proven by the realisation that it was a fulfilment of Zechariah 9:9:

"Rejoice greatly, O daughter of Zion; shout, O daughter of Jerusalem: behold, thy King cometh unto thee: he is just, and having salvation; lowly, and riding upon an ass, and upon a colt the foal of an ass."

All this is well known. The Messiah was here manifesting his kingship. "Behold, thy King cometh." I know that measured by human standards it was derisory – no doubt the Romans sniggered and turned away. A King in homespun cloth riding upon an ass. One day they will cast lots for his kingly garment. Matthew 21:10 says that, "all the city was moved". I took the trouble to look up that word "moved" and discovered an interesting thing. In the original it is the very same word as occurs in Matthew 27:51: "And, behold, the veil of the temple was rent in twain from the top to the bottom; and the earth did *quake,* and the rocks rent." The word "quake" is the one – "the city was *moved*". So let us not tone it down. It did cause a great stir – a minor earthquake: the crowds, the shouting, the excitement. As it appears to me, Jesus is compelling metropolitan Jerusalem to recognise his claim to kingship over Israel. The kingdom of heaven is at hand, and for one hour the King of that kingdom claimed their allegiance and their recognition.

Its purpose may also have this in it. Very soon he will be pronouncing doom over the city. With weeping eyes and tremulous voice he will say: "Your house is left unto you desolate" (Matthew 23:38). God never sends judgement without first giving opportunity to repent and turn back. Was this the final appeal of the Messiah? He did demonstrate his claim to government by going on to cleanse the temple. Just for one brief moment the centre of the city of God was made pure and beautiful by the Messiah. Remember Matthew 21:14: "And the blind and the lame came to him in the temple; and he healed them." For one brief moment the kingdom of heaven drew near. The robbers were banished and the temple was a house of prayer. In the midst of broken tables and money trampled underfoot, he healed the outcasts. The children are singing in the house of God for one hour of the kingdom. The record tells us something about the priests – it says: "they were sore displeased" (verse 15). So although I said at the beginning of this section it was derisory – I meant in the eyes of the Romans – yet it is true to say that, as far as we can tell, the whole city was stirred. The people were shaken. The business people, the priests, the common people, the Galileans, the children – they were all affected. Yes it was a minor earthquake.

Of course we must look at it in the long run. That section which in Zechariah began with "Thy King cometh" goes on eventually to say this:

"And his feet shall stand in that day upon the mount of Olives, which is before Jerusalem ... and there shall be a very great valley ... the earthquake in the days of Uzziah King of Judah ... and the LORD shall be King over all the earth: in that day and there shall be one LORD, and his name one."

So let us thank God for the King who came to claim his kingdom. Let nobody rob you of the vision of it – a kingdom which is real and substantial and has its metropolis at Jerusalem, the city of the great King. The children who sang will one day play in the streets thereof. This was the vision of the kingdom which filled the hearts of those people in Oxford eighty years ago with new hope. And I want to tell you this – all over the world I have seen faces aglow with joy when they talk of it. Hold it fast and let no man rob you of it.

Parables: the values of the kingdom

All this being in our minds we have now to turn to the great thirteenth chapter of Matthew's Gospel, a chapter full of things about the King's kingdom – all these parables which begin "the kingdom of heaven is likened unto ..." In the comparable passage in Mark these things are called "the mystery of the kingdom of God". A mystery in the Bible is not something mysterious but something at one time hidden and now disclosed. The disclosure is accomplished in this section by likening the kingdom of God to other things which throw light upon its nature. So the kingdom of God is like a man which sowed good seed in his field, but his enemy came and sowed tares among the wheat. Or it is like a grain of mustard seed which a man took and sowed in his field and eventually it became a tree in which the birds of the air lodged. Or the kingdom is like unto leaven which a woman used until the whole was leavened. Or it is like a hidden treasure in a field which a man sold all he had to buy. Or it is like a very precious pearl which a man sold all his other pearls to gain. Or it is like a dragnet cast into the sea which, when it is full, takes of every kind, good and bad.

This kingdom to come which will have its centre in Jerusalem and which will govern the whole world eventually with the Messiah as King – is it really like a field with good and bad seed, or mustard seed, or pearls in a field or leaven in a basin of dough? How shall we understand it rightly? I bring you to Matthew 21:

"When the lord therefore of the vineyard cometh, what will
he do unto those husbandmen? They say unto him, He will
miserably destroy those wicked men, and will let out his
vineyard unto other husbandmen, which shall render him
the fruits in their seasons. Jesus saith unto them, Did ye
never read in the scriptures, The stone which the builders
rejected, the same is become the head of the corner: this is
the Lord's doing, and it is marvellous in our eyes? Therefore
say I unto you, The kingdom of God shall be taken from you,
and given to a nation bringing forth the fruits thereof."

(verses 40-43)

Notice verse 43 especially. It reveals a solemn moment in the
history of the rulers of Israel. The kingdom was to be taken from
them and was to be given to another nation. These Jewish rulers
were to cease being the prospective aristocracy of the kingdom of
heaven; this high honour was to be bestowed upon others, who
Jesus calls "a nation". Now mark the qualification which justified
that new nation being chosen to receive this high honour. They
were to be given the kingdom because now they are already
bringing forth the fruits thereof. What does it mean – bringing
forth the fruits? Surely it means that they are people who
realise the kingdom principles in their lives now, who manifest
the kingdom values in their daily living and who proclaim the
kingdom fact to those around them. Notice they are called "a
nation". Now a nation is a group of people who have sworn
allegiance to one government, who have committed themselves
to obey one law and have freely given their loyalty to one leader.

So I put it to you that the nation to whom Jesus referred are
the people gathered about the Messiah, the living King, and are
instruments of his will and are under his discipline, submitting
to his commands and subject to his government. Confirmation
of this conclusion is found in the word of Peter the Apostle:

"But ye are a chosen generation, a royal priesthood, an holy
nation, a peculiar people; that ye should shew forth the
praises of him who hath called you out of darkness into his
marvellous light."   (1 Peter 2:9)

The great thing to remember is that the principles of the kingdom of God operate in their lives – hence they bring forth the fruits of the kingdom.

The values of the kingdom are the master principles which guide them. This is what Jesus meant by "seek ye first the kingdom of God, and his righteousness". The fruit of the kingdom is the righteousness which comes from seeking the kingdom. The Apostle Paul once wrote to the Roman ecclesia these words: "The kingdom of God is not meat and drink; but righteousness, and peace, and joy in the Holy Spirit" (Romans 14:17). Paul is stressing that eating or abstaining will not commend us to God, but by seeking the great values of righteousness and peace and joy. These are the master principles of the kingdom. The ecclesia of Christ is not the kingdom but there is a very vital connection between the one and the other – one is the nation of people dominated by the principles of the kingdom and seeking its values who consequently bring forth its fruits in readiness to inherit its life and its government. So Jesus says categorically: "Verily I say unto you, Whosoever shall not receive the kingdom of God as a little child shall in no wise enter therein." When he says "receive the kingdom of God", obviously he does not mean receive the actual kingdom, but receive the kingdom principles and the kingdom values. It is only humble submission to these principles now which entitles a man to abundant entrance into the kingdom in the age to come. As Jesus said, "… bringing forth the fruits thereof".

Now it is in this way that we must understand Matthew chapter 13. The sowing, the treasure, the pearl, the dragnet, the leaven, are telling us about the kingdom principles operating in life today as a probation for the receiving of the kingdom when the Messiah returns. So the principles of the kingdom of God are at work among men, provoking into growth and sifting and separating men and women from the world; helping them to overcome the forces which inhibit growth, helping them to bring forth fruit. The values of the kingdom are working from the smallest beginnings like the mustard seed, but eventually the harvest, largely unseen now, will one day be revealed as a great multitude out of all nations.

The work is not ostentatious but often quiet and unobstrusive, like the leaven, working slowly but persistently until the whole is leavened. So when a man finds the great pearl he has to be willing to exercise sacrifice and self-denial to gain the prize. He sells all he has to secure the true riches. These are the values of the kingdom imposed upon earthly thinking. So with the dragnet. The Gospel of the kingdom issues a challenge to the heart and the mind. It has the effect of making men to be outwardly what they are inwardly, and they are revealed as worldlings or as pilgrims. In the final assessment one is separated from the other. How they are separated at last is measured by how they valued the kingdom principles in the day of probation.

So these parables show us how that holy nation will be formed and will bring forth the fruits of the kingdom. Let us as we leave this section ponder the word of the Messiah in Matthew 13:

"Jesus saith unto them, Have ye understood all these things? They say unto him, Yea, Lord. Then said he unto them, Therefore every scribe which is instructed unto the kingdom of heaven is like unto a man that is an householder, which bringeth forth out of his treasure things new and old."

(Matthew 13:51,52)

I believe that the things new and things old are not two separate groups of things – one forever old and one forever new. I believe that they are the same things – once old and always new. Everything is new and everything is old. The principle is old, the application to ourselves is new. The root is old, the blossom is new. Destroy the old and there will be nothing new. Try to invent something new without reference to the old and it will wither and die. Notice Jesus says this is especially true about being instructed unto the kingdom of God. God grant you may feel it to be true and for your soul's sake, hold it fast. Amen.

4 |

Authority and power

IT would not have been sufficient to have put Authority alone. The essential thing is Authority with Power. Let me give you an illustration of this principle. A policeman can halt the busy traffic in a moment by raising his hand. That is authority. But the drivers have the power. They could if they liked drive on regardless. His arm could not stop one of them. So the policeman is authority without power, and the authority succeeds because it is conceded by those who come under it.

On the other hand, sometimes you have power without authority. For example, some dictator who has taken control because he has the tanks and the guns. He certainly has the power but he has no authority – constitutionally his power is unauthorised. But in the case of the King, he has authority supported by power – and it is this we have now to examine as Matthew has unveiled it.

First of all I bring you to Matthew 7:24: "Therefore whosoever heareth these sayings of mine, and doeth them, I will liken him unto a wise man, which built his house upon a rock ..." Jesus spoke about the man who hears the sayings he utters and obeys them, and says he is like a man who builds his house upon the rock and in the time of storm and tempest it stands. The man who hears and ignores is like a man who builds on the sand, and in the time of storm and tempest the house crumbles – the man is buried in the ruins of his own work. There is no middle course, no maybe, no perhaps one thing or the other, the words are emphatic and categoric.

"He taught them as one having authority"

What I would like you to notice is the comment of Matthew at the end of the chapter. Let us read it:

> "And it came to pass, when Jesus had ended these sayings, the people were astonished at his doctrine: for he taught them as one having authority, and not as the scribes."   (7:28,29)

The interesting thing is this. On the face of it you might think Matthew is saying that Jesus had authority and the scribes did not, but this is not the intention. As a matter of fact the scribes were full of authority – they were the most authoritarian people in the nation. That is not the comparison which Matthew is drawing attention to. The real comparison is this: Matthew is asking us to note the difference between the authority of the scribes and the authority of Jesus as the people sensed it. So let us try to notice what the difference was. The authority of the scribes was dogmatic, critical, censorious. They were ready to excommunicate and to ostracise. They held an official position which entitled them to lay down the law. Then again the authority of the scribes was by nature interpretive: they interpreted other men's teaching – the great rabbis of the past and the schools of the present.

You will remember at the time of Jesus there were two great schools of interpretation in Israel – the Shimei school and the Hillel school, and it was this that provoked the question to Jesus about divorce. There is nothing wrong in engaging in interpretation itself – it can be very valuable. But we must mark the nature of the interpretation. They could dogmatise about the length of a Sabbath day's journey or the length of a phylactery. They could dogmatise about what constituted work on the Sabbath day – a man rubs out a few grains of corn in his hand and they said he is working, he is threshing the corn. A lame man newly cured picks up his bed to walk home and they said he is labouring, he is carrying his bed. They knew a man has to honour his father and his mother but they worked out that if you dedicated the benefits in theory to the cause of God, you were free from the support of your parents. About these things they used their authority and they claimed attention because they had the authority of the state church behind them.

Now when the King spoke to the people they sensed that he also spoke with authority but that it was different from the scribes. He spoke confidently and categorically but he was no mere dogmatist. He taught without reference to other people and without fear or favour. The scribes, because of their official position, could claim to be heard; the King on the other hand could claim no right to be heard by reason of any official position – yet when he spoke, Matthew says the people were *astonished*. We know that soldiers were transfixed, priests and lawyers were compelled to confess his authority. The King's authority was not merely interpretive, though he often quoted from the prophets, and gave their words new meaning.

What was the nature of the power? What was it that constituted this authority? I am going to put it to you as it appears to me from the words of Matthew's Gospel. It was the self-evident truth of what he said. As he spoke, men were compelled to confess, 'Yes, that is true, that is true'. Even today you can find this sometimes: in the midst of complexity and confusion, one clear mind will voice the simple uncomplicated truth, and suddenly you know in your deepest heart that you have got to the centre of the matter. So it was with the King. It was not an opinion, it was the voice of origination. It was the final voice, the awe-inspiring authority of the voice of God.

So I put it to you what it was that constituted the nature of his authority. It was the self-evident truth of what he said, coupled with the personality of the one who spoke, confirmed by the signs which he did. Matthew saw this superlatively in the King and said: "He taught ... as one having authority." It carried conviction into this man's heart and on the page of his Gospel he confessed it.

I believe it is the authority of Kingship. Have you sensed it? Sometimes his words scorch us and sometimes they soothe us. As he speaks our reason is satisfied; our hearts are moved and so our will is energised. His word places God in the position of absolute and final supremacy: "Seek ye first the kingdom of God ... and all these things shall be added unto you." Do you not know that in your deepest heart? That is the only perspective that can satisfy us. To have gained the whole world and to have missed him and his kingdom is to have lost all. All the best material things are empty things and worthless things if they are to be secured at the cost of losing his comradeship and his fellowship.

Listen to his measurement of man: "Lay not up for yourselves treasure upon earth ... but lay up for yourselves treasure in heaven." He is telling us that man can only realise his true destiny, not by satisfying his senses only, but by living on the plane of the spiritual. He is saying something which we must hold to at all costs – that man is a spiritual creature, made in God's image and in some sense kin with Him.

According to the King man is able to realise his life most fully in possession of those things which are essentially part of the infinite life of God. Remember Luke 20 and the judgement he delivered upon the relative claims of Man and God. Recall the balanced and unanswerable way in which the truth was revealed. He said, "Show me a penny". If he had produced one himself the issue would have been blunted. They must show the penny. They did and said he, "Whose image and superscription is this?" Without a moment's hesitation they say "Caesar's". That was the moment when the answer was fashioned. The image was Caesar's and the penny was theirs – they were glad to use Caesar's things for their own advantage.

"Render therefore unto Caesar the things which be Caesar's, and unto God the things which be God's." The principle is this, that for the true man doing the second will ensure the first. Later on the New Testament writers will clearly develop the principle that obedience to the civil government is a faithful part of doing the will of God. The King declares that in all the forces of human life which might come to be declared Caesar's, his men must never forget that their first and final allegiance is to the throne of God. This means that they must seek to realise in the world the very values of the kingdom which they represent and of the King to whom they have given their unqualified loyalty.

Recall how he looks upon the restlessness of men. He does not say that anxiety is wrong. He knows that it is part of human nature to seek and to be anxious. He knows that this is the inspiration of endeavour and striving. But he draws our mind to what is important concerning the things about which we are anxious and after which we seek. To be anxious about the things which abide is the very ethic of the Gospel. "Seek ye first the kingdom of God ..." His view of life is that it is full and free and wonderful – only when all its varied ways and possibilities are related to the one centre of life, the throne of God.

This is the central passion of the Messiah's teaching. Then he declares that character is the vital thing. As we have seen already he places no blessing on having, even on doing, but on being. The man of character is greater than the man of property or the man of attainment. Now in this fundamental estimate of the King is there not the ring of absolute truth? To those who have accepted his Lordship he reveals the vital importance of influence and marks the kind of influence which men need most: "Ye are the salt of the earth"; "Ye are the light of the world."

Salt is pungent, antiseptic. It hurts when it is in the vicinity of the wound but at last it heals and saves and preserves. By its antiseptic nature it halts the spread of corruption.

Think of the power of light. Light flashes and flames and is not by any means welcome to the man who has something to hide, but in the end it is the only way to be led out of darkness and doom into liberty and freedom. Is not this the very science of life? We may hide the truth for a long time but in our deepest heart we know that one day we must bring it out into the light and confess it and repudiate it – and when that happens that is the day of freedom, restfulness and release.

I said that his word sometimes scorches us. He tells us that he who looks on sin with desire has committed it already in his heart. Do we not know that the King's estimate of guilt is absolutely true. We would if we could but for the present we cannot – and when men say that, are they not guilty? As a man "thinketh in his heart, so is he". His word cuts incisively like a knife through all our sophistry and all our guile. I know it and I confess it. We sometimes try to make wrong things right by giving them high sounding names and make them plausible, but in the presence of the King's measurement we are made to be openly what we are secretly. Our inwardness is brought out – not to destroy us, but at last to save us from ourselves.

Mark his measurement of righteousness. The scribes and the Pharisees sought to do right in order to sustain their reputation. They said it was important to be seen to be right. They said that they had a standard to uphold – a law to keep and fulfil. At its best it is a faulty motive because it is not strong enough to ensure righteousness when things are against it. With this motive a man may keep straight whilst all is well and whilst the sun shines, but in times of adversity or ridicule or if some alluring self-advancement can be gained only if the standard is compromised – then this motive will break down. Mark therefore the wisdom of the Messiah. "Except your righteousness shall exceed the righteousness of the scribes and Pharisees, ye shall in no case enter into the kingdom of heaven." The righteousness which exceeds is that which acts in response to the love of God and for the glory of God. For love's sake is the only force which will hold strong against all the insidious temptations to compromise. You will remember the old proverb, "Honesty is the best policy". The truth is that a man who is honest as a matter of policy is really a rogue at heart.

I once read of a man who said, 'My quarrel with Christ is that he is not practical. Christ said, "Love your enemies"; that is impractical, I cannot do that, it is beyond me'. It was doubtless an honest criticism. But the one to whom it was made said this: 'Suppose you could be brought to love your enemies – what then?' And the critic said, 'God help me, it would solve all the problems which curse humanity'. Why is that so interesting? Because it was a compulsive recognition of the authority of the King. That is all we need. I put it to you bluntly. Has he ever said a false thing? Has he ever said aught which we could overthrow? Where do we differ from his position? Where does our criticism commence? We know that all he says is designed to realise the glory of God and he is doing it by securing the salvation of men. Was there anything nobler? Is he not the Lord of the universe, the High Priest of humanity, the voice of God? All this is revealed in Matthew's Messiah.

Submission and responsibility

Let us pass on. Pursuing Matthew's insight into the King's authority I bring you to Matthew 8:

> "And when Jesus was entered into Capernaum, there came unto him a centurion, beseeching him, and saying, Lord, my servant lieth at home sick of the palsy, grievously tormented. And Jesus saith unto him, I will come and heal him. The centurion answered and said, Lord, I am not worthy that thou shouldest come under my roof: but speak the word only, and my servant shall be healed. For I am a man under authority, having soldiers under me: and I say to this man, Go, and he goeth; and to another, Come, and he cometh; and to my servant, Do this, and he doeth it. When Jesus heard it, he marvelled, and said to them that followed, Verily I say unto you, I have not found so great faith, no, not in Israel."
>
> (verses 5-10).

Let us mark it carefully. The centurion confessed that Jesus had the power to cure from a distance without standing in the very presence of the sickness itself. A faithful confession certainly, but was this the faith that excelled any other in the land of Israel?

If we read the same dialogue from Luke 7 we spot a difference. This is one of the cases I hinted at in the beginning where reference to another Gospel can illuminate Matthew. Here it is the extra word in verse 8 of Luke chapter 7. The word is "also". I ought to say that in the RV the word "also" is in Matthew as well. "For I *also* am a man set under authority, having under me soldiers, and I say unto one, Go, and he goeth; and to another, Come, and he cometh; and to my servant, Do this, and he doeth it." The word "also" is the supreme word. It reveals the centurion's insight and his faith. What he was saying was this: 'I perceive, Jesus, that you also are like me, under authority yourself and having under you those who you can command.' To the centurion this was, in the sphere of his upbringing, the highest ideal of life and when he looked at Jesus he saw it fulfilled in the noblest and finest sense. It was a recognition that true responsibility can be exercised only if there is first true submission. This the centurion saw in the King and he confessed it.

I think it was this that made Jesus marvel. I am not going to say that the centurion had formulated this idea as a result of long and deep thought and disputation. It may be that he had before never expressed it in words – but seeing it in the King he was compelled to put into words the method which controlled and regulated his own life.

Notice the philosophy is made up of two parts: the condition and the result. Submission is the condition; responsibility is the result. Think first of submission. "I am a man under authority": that is submission. "Having under me soldiers": that is responsibility. The Roman centurion submitted to the cause of the Roman Empire and that cause was personified in the Roman Emperor. All loyalty was submitted to the master person on the throne. What was submitted? Everything. The Roman soldier surrendered his will, his property, his relations, his time, his clothes, his food, all his ability. All this was submitted to the control of the master on the throne: his *sacramentum*.

What was the purpose of the submission? The Roman soldier submitted so as to make himself fit for his calling. The ultimate aim was the perfection of the one who submitted so that he could render true service to that to which he was called. Notice the responsibility, "Having under me soldiers". The centurion submits to the throne so that he himself may exert the authority of the throne over others for whom he is responsible. He said in effect, 'I submit to the authority of the empire so that I can represent the authority'. Those who wield authority must be in a right relationship with the source of the authority. The

Roman centurion perceived that what was true in his own life was true superlatively in the life of the King. This made Jesus marvel. The secret of true authority was spoken and applied by this Roman soldier. Christ was under authority – the authority of the great empire we call the kingdom of God, which was personified in God Himself, the sovereign, the ruler over the whole empire. He was a man under authority. "I do nothing of myself ... I do always the things which are pleasing to him." "My meat is to do the will of him that sent me, and to finish his work." It was a life under perfect and absolute authority. It was a life of perfect and absolute submission, and therefore it was a life responsible. "Having under me soldiers": that is to say, all the forces of the kingdom of God given into his hands over which he has control and authority. The authority he exercises is the authority to which he has submitted. This is the great principle which underlies the authority of the king, and which is ever applicable to all who at last would rule.

Listen to this from Revelation 2:26: "He that overcometh, and keepeth my works unto the end", that is submission; "to him will I give power (authority, RV) over the nations", that is responsibility. What men are going to be, is related directly to what they are. If at last any man wishes to hold the sceptre, he must first have bent and kissed it. This is the secret of the King's right to rule. Remember this: "Who being in the form of God ... made himself of no reputation, and took upon him the form of a servant ... and became obedient unto death, even the death of the cross" (Philippians 2:6-8); that is submission. "Wherefore God also hath highly exalted him, and given him a name which is above every name: that at the name of Jesus every knee should bow ... and that every tongue should confess that Jesus Christ is Lord, to the glory of God the Father" (verses 9,10); that is responsibility.

So the law of life which in a restricted sense motivated that Roman soldier, when it is magnified and glorified is at the very centre of the life of the King and eventually at the centre of the life of his disciples. The Roman soldier had authority over one hundred men; that is why he is called a centurion. The King claims authority at last over an unnumbered multitude who though diverse in many things, are alike in one thing: they have all kissed the sceptre, they have all bent the knee to the throne, they have all gladly submitted to the King's authority. At last they are to sing a great song upon Mount Zion:

> "Thou art worthy ... for thou wast slain, and hast redeemed us to God by thy blood ... and hast made us ... kings and priests: and we shall reign on the earth."

So that is the nature and the effect of the King's authority. It is not some arbitrary thing without sense or reason, it is based upon principle and upon forces which are divinely natural. And out of these very principles emerges the power which accompanies the authority. Crown the ideal and you have tapped the source of power.

Messiah's power

Finally in this section let us fix our minds upon the power of the Messiah as it is revealed in the Gospel of Matthew. Think of the splendid declaration when Jesus came and spoke to the disciples and said: "All power is given unto me in heaven and in earth" (Matthew 28:18). Now when you think about it that is the most comprehensive affirmation of power there can ever be. Notice it is *all power* – it is not partial, it is not selective. Nothing is excluded, nothing is qualified. And then its sphere of operation – in heaven and on earth. That is the universe. He is Lord of the universe.

In the Gospel of Matthew there are many examples of his power and I must confess it is difficult to know which to fix upon to ponder as an illustration, but in the end I settled for Matthew 9 to start with:

> "And he entered into a ship, and passed over, and came into his own city. And, behold, they brought to him a man sick of the palsy, lying on a bed: and Jesus seeing their faith said unto the sick of the palsy; Son, be of good cheer; thy sins be forgiven thee. And, behold, certain of the scribes said within

themselves, This man blasphemeth. And Jesus knowing their thoughts said, Wherefore think ye evil in your hearts? For whether is easier, to say, Thy sins be forgiven thee; or to say, Arise, and walk? But that ye may know that the Son of man hath *power* on earth to forgive sins, (then saith he to the sick of the palsy,) Arise, take up thy bed, and go unto thine house. And he arose, and departed to his house. But when the multitudes saw it, they marvelled, and glorified God, which had given such *power* unto men."   (verses 1-8)

Mark the words of the Messiah to the broken man: "Son, be of good cheer." You can be sure that Jesus is not telling the man to cheer up. That would be superficial. Cheering up lasts for a little while but then the old agony returns. No – the word "cheer" rightly translated is 'courage'. Jesus said, "Son be of good courage" and then forgave his sins and made him sound: "Take up thy bed, and go unto thine house". Those who saw it knew it was power – no half measures, no 'keep taking the tablets'. Some men's cures are gradual; this was instant and comprehensive. So they marvelled and gave glory to God which had given such power to man.

Now look down the chapter to verse 20:

"And, behold, a woman, which was diseased with an issue of blood twelve years, came behind him, and touched the hem of his garment: for she said within herself, If I may but touch his garment, I shall be whole. But Jesus turned him about, and when he saw her, he said, Daughter, be of good comfort; thy faith hath made thee whole. And the woman was made whole from that hour."   (verses 20-22)

The words that Jesus addressed to this suffering woman are exactly the same as to the paralysed man. I know it says, "Be of good comfort", but it is the same word as that translated "cheer". What he said to the woman was, "Be of good courage". The despairing agony of a suffering soul was ended in a moment. He said, "Thy faith hath made thee whole", but she was cured before he said it. Mark tells us why – she touched him and immediately he perceived that *power* had gone out of him.

Come now to Matthew 14 from verse 22 onwards. This you know well. The disciples are in a boat and they are enveloped by a storm. The waves were rough and the wind was contrary. Suddenly they see Jesus walking over the tempest-tossed sea. They are afraid and troubled; they think it is a phantom. Then he speaks to them and says (verse 27), "Be of good cheer; it is I; be not afraid". And afterwards there was a great calm. They were frightened by the unknown but by his *power* the storm and the fear were calmed.

In every case he spoke the same words: "Be of good courage", but what must interest us now is why they should have courage. In no case does Jesus seek to minimise the forces which caused them to be afraid or which brought suffering. In every case he recognised the reality of the things which assaulted the people in need. In every case he called upon them to have courage. Why should they have courage and why should he tell them this? Because in every case he placed his power between the assaulted person and the assaulting foe. It was the fact of Jesus himself that gave reason why they should take courage.

Go back over the cases and see if this is not true. The paralysed man who was steeped in sin. Jesus went to the heart of it – he stood between the man and his sin and with the authority of God said: "Thy sins be forgiven." Then he was able to speak the word of commanding power: "Take up thy bed, and go unto thine house." He dealt with the principle of evil out of which the man's condition had sprung and brought him restoration.

So it was with the poor woman stricken by a disease that not only brought suffering but excommunication – an issue of blood. "Someone touched me", he said, "for I perceive that power has gone out of me." That was the reason for courage. His power came between her and her awful disability. Her pain was cancelled and her fear was banished.

Do you know that the Greek word translated "virtue" in the KJV and "power" in other versions, that which went out of him and came between the woman and her sickness, is the Greek word *dunamis* (anglicised as 'dynamite'). Think of those men in peril on the sea – frightened and bewildered. Notice what he said: "Be of good cheer; it is I." The fact of Jesus himself was the answer to their foreboding. "It" – that is the phantom, the mystery – "is I". He came between them and their fears, terror, and trauma. A dimmed vision of their Lord had turned him into a phantom, but when he spoke they knew him and there came a great calm. They said, "Of a truth thou art the Son of God".

So ponder it. As we look reverently at this majestic figure who moves through the Gospel narrative of Matthew and in whose footsteps we cannot truly place ours for he walks too certainly for that, let us be sure in our hearts that he is a man of infinite authority and unlimited power. He is the King, to whom is given all power in heaven and earth. For those who have faith, he still speaks the words, "Be of good courage", and it means that finally he puts himself between the believing disciple and all the forces which left to ourselves could doom us. God grant you may know it to be true.

The Messiah rejected
Matthew 26:57-68

I N this section our first step must be, quickly and therefore
briefly, to trace the process of rejection as it is revealed by
Matthew. Then we shall seek to retrace our steps and look at
some evidence more incisively. So let us begin at the beginning
and notice where the first sign of rejection emerges according
to Matthew. It is in chapter 9 and through an incident we have
already considered: verses 2-8, the case of the paralysed man.
The King was a man who always measured the physical in terms
of the spiritual. He heard the birds sing and said, 'Your heavenly
Father feeds them'; he saw the flowers on the hillside and said,
'God clothes them'; he handled a common loaf and said, 'There is
a bread which men may eat and live for ever'.

So it is with the paralysed man. He saw a connection
between the physical and the spiritual. The man was burdened
by his sin – Christ knew it and dealt with the evil out of which the
man's limitation had come. "Son, be of good cheer; thy sins be
forgiven thee" (9:2). The measurement of the scribes was, "This
man blasphemeth" (verse 3). Notice carefully their estimate of
Jesus – a blaspheming rabbi. We shall have need to return to it
before long.

This was the first rupture with the leaders according to
Matthew. Then in verses 10-15 we have the Pharisees objecting
that Jesus was consorting with publicans and sinners – and the
reply of the Messiah with unanswerable logic: "They that be
whole need not a physician, but they that are sick" (verse 12).
"But go ye and learn what that meaneth, I will have mercy and

not sacrifice: for I am not come to call the righteous, but sinners to repentance" (verse 13).

They could not have liked it and must have been nursing resentment. In verses 32-34 Jesus heals a dumb man possessed with a devil. The Pharisees' reaction is, "He casteth out devils through the prince of the devils" (verse 34). Diabolism is a very serious charge. Notice it at this stage – it marks the development of the estrangement.

Growing opposition
Go now to Matthew chapter 12, verses 1-8. Here we have the case of the disciples rubbing out the corn in their hands on the Sabbath day. The Pharisees objected that they were doing what was not lawful on the Sabbath. The reply of the King must have been particularly galling for them. He said, "Have ye not read what David did ...?" (verse 3), and, "Have ye not read in the law ...?" (verse 5) or, "If ye had known what this meaneth ... ye would not have condemned the guiltless" (verse 7). To be rebuffed by an appeal to the very law in which they were the experts must have touched their professional pride. Then the final thrust: "The Son of man is Lord even of the sabbath day" (verse 8).

Then in verses 9-14 we have the case of the man with the withered hand. Jesus cured him in the synagogue on the Sabbath day. He argued that they would save a sheep on the Sabbath; why was it wrong to save a man? They could not get away from the fact that the action of Jesus was justified by their own behaviour on the Sabbath. Notice the outcome: "Then the Pharisees went out, and held a council against him, how they might destroy him" (verse 14). Now the opposition is taking a much more sinister direction. They have resolved to destroy him.

Continuing in verses 22-30, Jesus casts out the demons of blindness and dumbness. The Pharisees heard it and said that it was the work of Beelzebub, the prince of devils.

In verses 38-42, certain of the scribes and Pharisees seek a sign from the King. His reply indicts them squarely: "An evil and adulterous generation seeketh after a sign; and there shall no sign be given to it, but the sign of the prophet Jonas" (verse 39). The word "adulterous" must have upset them deeply, for they knew that it was used in the Old Testament to describe the very lowest condition of the people of God when they had departed from their high calling into the very worst condition of degradation and infidelity – a spiritual harlot. So as they had refused every other sign they must wait for the sign of Jonah – a man who came out of death to proclaim the word of God.

We move on to chapter 15, verses 1-20. Here a special deputation of Pharisees and scribes came from Jerusalem to enquire, so it seemed, about the teaching of the Man from Nazareth. They were concerned about washing hands. His reply revealed that they ought to be concerned about how they selfishly shattered the second commandment, Honour thy father and mother. It was a conflict between tradition and truth. The Pharisees were offended – that was the disciples' estimate, putting it mildly (see verse 12). The metropolitan deputation must have been livid. He called them hypocrites and used Isaiah to prove their worship was false.

Chapter 16, verses 1-5. This time the Pharisees join with the Sadducees to tempt Jesus. He says they can discern the signs of the weather but are blind to the signs of the times. He calls them hypocrites, and left them.

Chapter 21, verses 12-17. In this passage Matthew reveals that the King moves to Jerusalem to enter the city as King, in fulfilment of the prophecy of Zechariah. Then he moves to the temple of God and clears out the forces of pollution and corruption. The blind and the lame were healed, the children proclaimed the Messiah and the priests were sore displeased; that means they were angry – angry men ready to plan mischief.

Chapter 21, verses 23-27. The chief priests and the elders challenge the authority of the King. He counters by asking them to declare themselves concerning John the Baptist (verse 25). It was a telling question because if they admitted that John was true and from God, they had to admit that so was Jesus, for John was Jesus' herald and testified of his authority. To accept one, made it illogical to reject the other. When John ceased Jesus took up the ministry.

They saw the dilemma and gave a dishonest answer: "We know not" – an admission of their wilful blindness. What a shambles – to be forced to admit ignorance about something of which they should have been certain. Can you imagine their inward wrath?

Chapter 23 is perhaps best known of all. It is a terrible indictment by the Messiah of the religious leaders of Israel. He calls them blind guides, fools, hypocrites, whited sepulchres, murderers of the prophets with blood on their hands, serpents and offspring of vipers. The terrible words are spoken in deep sorrow, for the passage ends with the King weeping over the city which had been brought to reject him by the very forces which he had been compelled to condemn with such telling and awful damnation. "Woe unto you", he said – his voice is choked with tears. "Woe unto you."

The outcome of this final and awful indictment of the rulers is discovered in chapter 26:

"And it came to pass, when Jesus had finished all these sayings, he said unto his disciples, Ye know that after two days is the feast of the passover, and the Son of man is betrayed to be crucified. Then assembled together the chief priests, and the scribes, and the elders of the people, unto the palace of the high priest, who was called Caiaphas, and consulted that they might take Jesus by subtilty, and kill him. But they said, Not on the feast day, lest there be an uproar among the people."

(verses 1-5)

The developing campaign of hatred has come to its climax. They resolved to kill him – for them there was no other remedy. So the Messiah is rejected by the people of God.

There are many questions which emerge from the consideration of how the Messiah was rejected – but there is one which I feel we ought to pursue more intensely in the interests of seeking to understand better Matthew's Messiah.

The culpability of the Jewish leaders

Why were the Pharisees, scribes, priests, rulers so blameworthy and deserving of such awful condemnation? In pursuit of that I want to bring you back to one of the incidents we have recollected already. The case of the man with the withered arm in chapter 12:

> "And when he was departed thence, he went into their synagogue: and, behold, there was a man which had his hand withered. And they asked him, saying, Is it lawful to heal on the sabbath days? that they might accuse him. And he said unto them, What man shall there be among you, that shall have one sheep, and if it fall into a pit on the sabbath day, will he not lay hold on it, and lift it out? How much then is a man better than a sheep? Wherefore it is lawful to do well on the sabbath days. Then saith he to the man, Stretch forth thine hand. And he stretched it forth; and it was restored whole, like as the other. Then the Pharisees went out, and held a council against him, how they might destroy him."
>
> (verses 9-14)

Let us read the details carefully. This is a crucial incident because the outcome was a clear resolution on the part of the Pharisees to destroy Jesus. I now use the right which I reserved in the beginning to look occasionally at another Gospel in order to illuminate the record of Matthew. I bring you to Mark chapter 3:

> "And he entered again into the synagogue; and there was a man there which had a withered hand. And they watched him, whether he would heal him on the sabbath day; that they might accuse him."
>
> (verses 1,2)

Notice the phrase, "And they watched him". It says they were watching him to see whether he would heal on the Sabbath day. It is probable that this paralysed man was a regular visitor to the synagogue – perhaps he had been coming for years. Evidently they knew that he would be there; he was there every Sabbath. They knew that the Man of Nazareth was coming too: indeed he was being set up on this particular Sabbath. It was all arranged. They wanted to trap him so that they might accuse him. That was the master plan. I dare say that the man had been guided to a place where he would in the synagogue come face to face with the Nazarene in such a way as to make his disability evident.

What is so interesting here is the thinking of the Pharisees. They were saying to themselves, 'If only we can get this disabled man into the presence of the Man from Nazareth, it is almost certain that he will want to help him, that he will attempt a cure. Then we shall have him'. Mark it well – the success of their plan rested on their acknowledgement that if this Man from Nazareth was confronted with a sick man he would not be able to restrain his compassion, even though it was the Sabbath day. They depended upon Jesus being true to his calling. Of all the people in the synagogue they knew that Jesus was the most dependable when it came to helping the undone. So they were saying, 'He will never be able to resist it. The trap is set'. Is it not interesting what an accurate estimate they had formed of the Messiah. What a compliment they paid him, without willing it.

We know what happened. He challenged them and said, "Is it lawful to do good on the sabbath day, or to do evil?" They said nothing – they did not wish to discourage him nor did they want to be accused of encouraging him. The true answer would have been: it is right to do good, it is wrong to do evil – but they would bear no such testimony. He said to the poor broken man, "Stand forth", and then with one superb command he gave him ability for his disability. The man surrendered and the power was communicated. Matthew says the hand was restored whole like the other.

The man must have been delighted. All the years of paralysis ended in one blinding flash on the Sabbath: the day God made for man. Jesus must have been well pleased – he had been able to do the work of God on God's day, to turn weakness into power, sorrow into joy, uselessness to usefulness. The Pharisees were glad too, but for different reasons. Their hope of the Nazarene had been fulfilled: he had proved true to their estimate of him. They depended upon him to heal and he had healed and restored. Their gladness was centred in the possibility of doing harm to the cause of the man who claimed to be Messiah. Their joy was in the chance to accuse and destroy. They were glad that he had violated the Sabbath as they saw it. They would have been disappointed if he had conformed to their view of doing right. It shows that they were not really interested in the upholding of right; they were not really concerned that God's law should be respected. Their overriding desire was that this man should be in a position where he could be indicted and destroyed. They were glad that, measured by their measurement, evil had been done.

They were not glad for the paralysed man. That he had been cured was to them of no consequence That half a lifetime of withered paralysis had been ended gave them no thankful satisfaction. No wonder Jesus was angry. Mark says he was angry, and more – he says he was grieved for the hardness of their heart.

It was the same with the man who was healed at the pool of Bethesda. They complained that he had carried his bed on the Sabbath. They were not concerned that thirty-eight wintry years of hopelessness had been ended.

So here is the point: the real blameworthiness and the real culpability of these men lies in the fact that they recognised that this Man from Nazareth was doing good and was saving the broken and the bruised and the bereft. They depended upon his compassion – they recognised his sympathetic understanding for those in need. They admitted his love, mercy and kindness. And yet in the face of that they condemned him. In the presence of the light they preferred darkness. Even at last when he was brought to the cross by their conspiracy, as they taunted him they said, "He saved others, himself he cannot save". Even in their attempt to mock him they had to concede that he had saved others.

This I submit was their awful culpability. And it is fixed in one word in the record in Mark 3: "the *hardness* of their hearts." Hardened hearts result in deceived hearts. In the presence of the best, the noblest, the purest and the most compassionate exhibition of divine life, they hardened their hearts. They admitted it, depended upon it and rejected it.

This is their awful indictment. This was their terrible sin. They loved darkness rather than light. And it was intensified by the fact that their high principles could be violated so easily when it suited them. This is the very point that Jesus made. "What man shall there be among you, that shall have one sheep, and if it fall into a pit on the sabbath day, will not lay hold on it, and lift it out?" (Matthew 12:11). Notice the words carefully: "What man ... that shall have one sheep." The argument is that you rescue it because it is yours. You are the owner and because of that you say that nothing should stand in the way of recovering your own in danger, even on the Sabbath. Now notice the implication. "How much then is a man better than a sheep?" He is saying that what you do for your sheep on the Sabbath, God does for His men on the Sabbath. What you recover for yourself, He recovers for Himself – Sabbath or not. This is part of their blameworthiness. They were willing to deny God what they insisted on for themselves. The answer to their hardness and their selfishness and their hypocrisy is in one command ringing through the synagogue: "Stretch forth thine hand."

The final rejection

Let us come now to the final incidents in the long process of the Messiah rejected. When you think of western constitutions which give protection and justice to all those who are accused before the law, there is perhaps in your mind one word which expresses comprehensively the force of the provisions – that word is 'equity'. When we turn to the case of the Man of Nazareth and the methods used by his accusers, there is one word which comes to mind to express the process by which he was tried – that word is 'perversion'. Brother Melva Purkis in his book *A Life of Jesus* proves that everything about the trial of the Messiah was illegal. The arrest, the trial itself, the cross-questioning, the evidence, were all illegal. The provisions to ensure justice for the Jew accused before the court were all violated. The Roman trial was more regulated. Under Roman law there had to be an accusation, then a cross-examination, then a defence, after which the verdict was given. In the trial before the Sanhedrin, the Jewish court, the witnesses made a bad showing. Caiaphas must have been on edge. He says to Jesus, "Answerest thou nothing? what is it which these witness against thee?" Then regaining his composure he finds a way out of his dilemma. Never mind that it is contrary to the law. In a loud voice he says: "I adjure thee by the living God, that thou tell us whether thou be the Christ, the Son of God." You know the reply of the King: "Thou hast said", which means, 'thou hast said the truth'. "Hereafter shall ye see the Son of man sitting of the right hand of power, and coming in the clouds of heaven." Caiaphas rent his clothes – an outer sign of inner shock and sadness. Of course, there was no real sadness, only a great deal of real satisfaction. He said: "He hath spoken blasphemy; what further need have we of witnesses? Behold, now ye have heard his blasphemy. What think ye?" The answer was a foregone conclusion: "He is guilty of death." The trial was over.

The important thing to mark is that the accusation was blasphemy and for this the accused was condemned. What we have to do is to look a little more incisively at the forces behind the accusation to see what really was driving this man, the high priest, to indict and condemn the Man of Nazareth, who we know was the best and the kindest man that ever lived. Remember something they said in the Council: "What do we? for this man doeth many miracles. If we let him thus alone, all men will believe on him: and the Romans shall come and take away both our place and nation" (John 11:47,48). "Then from that day forth they took counsel together for to put him to death" (verse 53).

Here we have touched the reality. They concluded that if his teaching progressed, their reign was over. His teaching made religion a thing of the heart, not of rabbinical learning. His teaching brought the sinner close to God and the broken spirit within reach of the healing compassion of divine love. This made nonsense of that ritual regularity which erected a barrier between the sinner and the love of God. Their condemnation of him was spoken in these words: "This man receiveth sinners, and eateth with them" (Luke 15:2). Mark it well then – the real ground of opposition to Jesus was hatred of the light, but we have seen that it was not the reason they put forward. Eventually it will be public zeal, patriotism, loyalty.

Of course this is nothing new, but in this case it was intensified. What could be purer and more godly than to root out an influence which blasphemed the holy name of God? What more noble calling than to protect the nation and save the inheritance? It sounds splendid, but we know it was all hollow and superficial and empty. The real accusation was that this man was a danger as they saw it to their position, their influence and their power. The purpose is the destruction of the Man of Nazareth but Caiaphas justified it for the loftiest of reasons: "It is expedient", he said, "that one man should die for the people, and that the whole nation perish not" – a great truth spoken in words of a shameful falsehood.

Let us pass on to the Roman part of the trial. They took their prisoner to Pilate early in the morning. Early though it was, he was up and about, probably because he knew they were coming. It is to me fascinating to try to estimate human nature as it is revealed to us in characters exposed in the word of God. I do not propose to go over all the details of the interrogation because you know them well. Let us notice how the accusation changed in the course of the journey from Caiaphas to Pilate.

In the Jewish court it was blasphemy but they knew Pilate would have none of that, so before him this is what they said:

"We found this fellow perverting the nation, and forbidding to give tribute to Caesar, saying that he himself is Christ a King ... He stirreth up the people, teaching throughout all Jewry, beginning from Galilee to this place."   (Luke 23:2,5)

So now the accusation is sedition. Blasphemy Pilate could ignore but sedition he could not. He examines Jesus but is unconvinced that he is a rebel or even dangerous. As we examined the motives of Caiaphas so we need to look at Pilate. What a sadly strange man he is: a melancholy example of vacillation and instability. He was strong in the sense that he had power; he was weak in the sense that he was cruel, selfish and cowardly. Power used in conjunction with those forces results almost certainly in disaster at last. Power may corrupt but it corrupts much more those who are already polluted.

Mark it well. First of all he blames the priests and then he admits that he after all is responsible. He washes his hands and then says: "Knowest thou not that I have power to crucify thee ...?" He pronounces Jesus innocent and then hands him over to be crucified. And yet we have heard of this before. He is a man knowing what is right and doing what is wrong. Why is he so pitiably weak? because there are things in his own life which tie his hands. There was the past guilt and the past failure. He had come under censure before; he has now to be extra careful not to invite it again. These circumstances have in them evident causes of personal danger for himself. After all, a man must think of himself sometimes. He wanted to do right but could not.

It has happened since. Sometimes men know what is right and what they ought to do, but they dare not do it because to do so would reveal them as hypocrites. Sometimes men know they ought to speak out and uphold the truth, but they dare not for to do so would show them to be uttering empty platitudes measured by their own life. Think of the agony of it. He knew why they had delivered the man from Galilee – "he knew that for envy they had delivered him". He knew he ought to release him but for reasons of self-interest and self-preservation he dare not. Sometimes men have to do what is right and take the consequence. To the vacillating man, beset by fear, all things seem alterable, changeful, unfixed.

So he parleyed, argued, debated, until the verdict of his own intellect was in a turmoil. He had listened to the priests, he had listened to the people, he had listened to his own wife and he had listened to Jesus – and then with that cheerlessness of soul which descends upon those who conclude that nothing is certain, he asks, "What is truth?" It was not spoken in jest, nor to gain information – it was spoken in scepticism and despair. Any man who violates his conscience is a man in tormented perplexity. His conviction was that Jesus was innocent. He knew the Pharisees were persecuting a guiltless man. He knew that the claim to royalty was nothing like sedition. The charge and the accusation had fallen to the ground. He was a Roman Procurator – he saw it – but he tried to get rid of his clear duty. The accusers were vocal and insistent. They did not like the candour of the Roman Governor about the suspected man. So, just as it was in the Sanhedrin trial, at the moment when the verdict was in the balance they played their trump card: "If thou let this man go, thou art not Caesar's friend." Pilate saw through their blackmail but dare not resist it. You might think at first sight that Pilate was the judge and Jesus was the prisoner, but the truth will reverse the positions: Jesus was the judge and Pilate was the prisoner – a man for the ages to pity and for the world to despise; a man whose name and fortune have been memorialised in one short, sad sentence, all down the centuries – He "suffered under Pontius Pilate".

So he went out and pronounced sentence upon a man of unblemished life, who was born to proclaim the truth. Thus the Messiah was rejected.

The Messiah exalted
Matthew 28

O NE thing ought to make us marvel as we come to this
final consideration about Matthew's Messiah. It is this
– the reserve of Matthew as he records the exaltation of
the King. Carefully and reverently he recorded his entombment.

There is something to marvel at here. Two men of whom
we know little, took it upon themselves to retrieve his body
and to bury him. Two secret disciples, at the end found their
courage and boldly went to Pilate and asked for the Lord's body.
The apostles who had companied with him, in the good days and
in the bad, through the zenith and through the decline, who
wanted to sit on his throne and had been promised twelve places
of supreme authority – they were not at the burial. Not many
attended the funeral: just these two secret disciples and two
Marys – Mary of Magadala and Mary the mother of James and
Joses. They stayed and they watched to the end. Four people at
the funeral of the Messiah.

The Lord's burial
It is not uncommon to attend the burial of someone you have
reason to love and through whom your life has been changed.
There were many who had good reason for being there –
measured by our western ways. Where were Lazarus and Martha
and Mary? What about the widow of Nain? Jairus and his girl?
The bridegroom of Cana? Unfair to ask it? Yes, no doubt. It is
Passover time. But what a strange thing it is: a man who had
helped so many, who had brought joy and solace to so many

hearts, upon whose words the weary had rested – at his end just two men and two women.

But notice this, they were the gentlest and most attentive people of all. They wrapped the body of the King in clean linen and laid it in the tomb.

As you read between the lines, do you not gather a sense of the gentle reverence with which they executed this last solemn duty? He had been bruised and broken by wicked hands. Sin became exceedingly sinful and in the conflict he was mauled by the brutality of the infamous. With obscene lips they blasphemed and spat upon his face. But once the victory was won, once the Armageddon of the ages had been fought and the triumph assured, then God allowed no hand of infamy to touch him.

The Psalmist had said, "Thou wilt not suffer thine Holy One to see corruption", and no corrupting power was allowed to interfere with his burial. With gentle hands moved by love they wrapped him and laid him. Every defiling power was excluded. Every polluted association was outlawed. God allowed no longer the forces of sin to defile the temple of his body. Nor did any eye set on him but the eyes of those who were destined to share his glory. Such was the concern of the Father for the Son.

On a point of accuracy and for the sake of any to whom it may not be clear, notice that Joseph "rolled a great stone to the door of the sepulchre, and departed" (Matthew 27:60). Every word is important – the word "rolled" is accurate. The stone was round and large like a millstone and as the sepulchre was properly prepared, the stone moved in a groove which sloped towards the tomb entrance. Joseph rolled the stone towards the other end of the groove and consequently across the hole of the entrance. Once it was in position it could be blocked and in any case it was much harder to move the stone away than to move it into position, because to move it away was to have to move it uphill along the groove. Hence when the women came the day after the Sabbath to continue the embalming they said, "Who shall roll us away the stone from the door of the sepulchre?" (Mark 16:3). They could not do it, they did not have the strength. So when

Matthew says that Joseph departed, this is how the sepulchre was left.

The next day at the instigation of the Pharisees, Pilate agreed to the sepulchre being made sure, setting a watch and sealing the stone. This is likely to mean that clay was plastered over the stone's edge and the border of the cave, and into the clay the pressing of a seal to ensure that it could not be interfered with in secret and without authorisation. Then the guarding by the soldiers.

Pause for a moment to ponder this. Was there ever such an exhibition of impotence? Seals and soldiers to watch the body of a dead man. If you are willing to concede that there is laughter in heaven there must have been laughter in heaven. They thought they were being shrewd; Gabriel must have smiled. In spite of all their precautions to stop the body being stolen, he left the tomb of his own volition.

"The angel of the Lord descended from heaven"

Matthew records something which as it appears to me is wonderfully inspiring:

"And, behold, there was a great earthquake: for the angel of the Lord descended from heaven, and came and rolled back the stone from the door, and sat upon it." (Matthew 28:2)

Here is the part that is so splendid. The angel "rolled back the stone ... and *sat* upon it". Angels do not sit. They have no need to sit. Have you ever read in the Bible of angels sitting? Remember to Zacharias there appeared an angel standing on the right side of the altar of incense. The angel said, "I am Gabriel that *stand* in the presence of God ..." (Luke 1:11,19). "Two men *stood* by them in white apparel; which also said, Ye men of Galilee ..." (Acts 1:10,11). John said: "I saw four angels *standing* on the four corners of the earth ..." (Revelation 7:1). Cornelius said, "A man [an angel] *stood* before me in bright clothing ..." (Acts 10:30).

But this time the angel *sat*. He rolled away the stone and then *sat* upon it. It seems to me there is a significance in this. The stone was man's invention to keep the body of Jesus in the tomb – sealed and guarded. Now to sit upon something is to demote it, to devalue it, to diminish it. By sitting, the angel from heaven was saying that Roman power is rejected, that Jewish priesthood is rejected, that human culture is rejected. The forces which were intent upon the destruction of the Messiah are spoiled and finished. It was a splendid gesture from heaven of the fact that is described by Peter: "This Jesus hath God raised up ... being by the right hand of God exalted ..." (Acts 2:32,33). This resurrection was a raising to exaltation. Others had been raised from death but this was different. This Jesus hath God raised up: this man who was rejected by men is accepted by God. The Creator is saying in the sight of all humanity that this man alone is acceptable to Him and that no others can be acceptable unless they join themselves with the exalted one. This one man alone receives the approbation of the Father in heaven. His life as the Messiah is at last sealed by the empty tomb, the sitting angel and the earthquake. This man's victory was won on the cross that the Greeks said was foolishness, the Hebrews said was *anathema*, and the world said was empty and useless.

The resurrection of the Messiah is saying to them – you are the foolishness, you are under the curse, you are empty and without power: the true attestation of the fact that what men in their folly thought was useless is the one thing through which their ultimate redemption is to be accomplished. No human eyes ever witnessed the resurrection, but no human being can ever escape its effect.

Early on that morning after the Sabbath, something remarkable happened in the garden. The clothes were undisturbed, but he was gone. The Prince of life among the dead. Out of the tomb and past the guards, in a moment in the twinkling of an eye, the man who is visible and invisible, he is gone. Old death riding on his pale horse is vanquished – left breathless. This is what the angel said: "... Jesus which was crucified. He is not here ..." They wanted to keep him there at all costs, lock him in the grave, forget him. But the angel said, "He is not here".

Matthew says that the keepers "became as dead men". There is a nice irony here. The one who they certified as dead is alive and is gone, and those who were sure that they were alive became as dead men. No wonder the angel asked, "Why seek ye the living among the dead?" Marvel then at the reserve of Matthew.

Let us retrace our steps and look again at some of the things recorded by Matthew. "And behold, there was a great earthquake" (28:2). Because this reference to the earthquake occurs in verse 2 we should not suppose that it actually occurred after the events recorded in verse 1. That is, we should not think that the earthquake happened after the women had arrived at the sepulchre. Verse 2 is in parenthesis – an interpolation, to explain the presence of the angel when the women reached the garden. Sometime during the night, towards dawn perhaps, the angel came. Matthew says "his countenance was like lightning, and his raiment white as snow". Human minds are compelled to use human syllables to describe the indescribable. Strong men, men of iron, Roman soldiers, they were part of the garrison seconded to the Jewish authorities during the feast to keep order; so not the temple guard, but part of the centurion's company on special duty for the Passover. Men of steel nerves and hard resolution. These men were terrified. They were filled with fear – as Matthew tells it, they fainted with fear. Like dead men they were. Later on when they come to tell what happened, not one of the authorities who heard them sought to cast any doubt upon their story. Nobody said they must have been dreaming or they had been deceived. It must have been evident that something terrible had happened to these steel-nerved soldiers.

So they gave large money to them to invent a story. It must have been large indeed, because it is not easy to persuade a Roman soldier to admit that he was asleep on duty. Indeed, in normal circumstances such an admission would result in court martial and death.

They did not think out the invented story very well. Have you noticed how foolish it was? "His disciples came by night, and stole him away while we slept" (verse 13). If they were asleep how would they know what happened and if they awoke just as the disciples were leaving they, the soldiers, could easily have caught them struggling with a corpse.

When people are desperate it often happens that the pressure of the anxiety leads them into childish folly which under calmer circumstances they would never dream of following. Notice Matthew is careful to say that the fainting of the soldiers was through *fear of him*, the angel, not through fear of the earthquake. They were paralysed through fear by the sight of the angel. Perhaps when he went into the tomb they gathered such strength as they could muster and crept away in terror to report their experience. So the blinding glory of the man from heaven was to some a cause of fear – and to others a cause of comfort and assurance.

"Then the eleven disciples went away into Galilee, into a mountain where Jesus had appointed them. And when they saw him, they worshipped him: but some doubted. And Jesus came and spake unto them, saying, All power is given unto me in heaven and in earth. Go ye therefore, and teach all nations, baptizing them in the name of the Father, and of the Son, and of the Holy Spirit: teaching them to observe all things whatsoever I have commanded you: and, lo, I am with you alway, even unto the end of the world. Amen."

(Matthew 28:16-20)

I submit we are entitled to seek illumination of this poignant incident from the Acts of the Apostles: "And when he had spoken these things, while they beheld, he was taken up; and a cloud received him out of their sight" (Acts 1:9).

The ascension

Although Matthew does not record it, I think we are entitled to feel that after the last word of his Gospel we may think next of the ascension. Perhaps it was no ordinary cloud which received him out of their sight. It has been suggested it was the cloud of the *Shekinah* glory of God, which was seen by Abraham, and Moses, and David, and Hezekiah, and Elijah, and Elisha, and

Peter, James and John on Horeb's height, and which John saw again on Patmos. It would be appropriate – it seems right – not an ordinary cloud but one rich with the glory of the Father. When Jesus comes again it will be with clouds and with the Father's glory.

Notice the first thing the Messiah did when he came to heaven: he sent two angels to earth. He said to them: 'Go and comfort those men of mine at Bethany – say to them':

"Ye men of Galilee, why stand ye gazing up into heaven? this same Jesus, which is taken up from you into heaven, shall so come in like manner as ye have seen him go into heaven."

(Acts 1:11)

Did he not know that the first moments of separation are the most intense and the most severe? Matthew records that Jesus said to them: "And, lo, I am with you alway, even unto the end of the world [age]."

We do not often speak of the ascension, but it is coupled inseparably with the resurrection. It is the highest manifestation of the exaltation of the Messiah. That this is so is shown from the words of Paul to the Ephesians:

"Now that he ascended, what is it but that he also descended first into the lower parts of the earth? He that descended is the same also that ascended up far above all heavens, that he might fill all things."   (Ephesians 4:9,10)

What is meant by Paul when he says, "He also descended first into the lower parts of the earth"? I would think that the words which best define it are in Philippians chapter 2: "And being found in fashion as a man, he humbled himself, and became obedient unto death, even the death of the cross" (verse 8). That is the descension because it is rock bottom. You cannot get lower than that.

Think of the shame of it. When we read Matthew chapter 26 we knew it was not refined, it was vulgar: the death of the pure and spotless by the hands of lawless men. Alone he trod the winepress. Being in the form of God, nevertheless he descended and came to rest in the lower parts of the earth. He was numbered among the transgressors. We must interpret the ascension by measuring the descension. By this the disorder was ended. The pollution was halted, the sin is cancelled.

Here is the wonder. As the light of the glorious resurrection of the Messiah is flashed upon it, the brutal cross is revealed as the trysting place where broken men can be remade, and where there is pardon, peace and purity for the undone. Here the polluted are blood-sprinkled and purified. As Paul tells it in Philippians 2, remember the next word after "the death of the cross". "Wherefore." This is the word which joins the descension to the ascension. It is the bridge between the past and the present and all that by the grace of God is to be accomplished in the future.

Highly exalted

Matthew records that Jesus said, "All power is given unto me in heaven and in earth". What a splendid affirmation of intent. So Paul says: "Wherefore God also hath highly exalted him, and given him a name which is above every name ..." "Wherefore", because the disorder is ended and the pollution is halted and the sin is cancelled and the curse of death is vanquished.

"Wherefore God also hath highly exalted him, and given him a name which is above every name: that at the name of Jesus every knee should bow, of things in heaven, and things in earth, and things under the earth; and that every tongue should confess that Jesus Christ is Lord, to the glory of God the Father."   (Philippians 2:9-11)

So the name that was bestowed upon him through the angel, the old hero name of Joshua, the name of the boy next door, is bestowed upon him again in heaven. God the Father is saying, 'My Son alone, the beloved, he has fulfilled the name'.

In Ephesians chapter 1 Paul wrote that God "set him at his own right hand in the heavenly places". The right hand of God is the most exalted place in the whole of the universe. It is the place of infinite and unfading glory: the place where weariness is unknown; where weakness never comes; where darkness is banished. He was subjected to weakness here – he has all power there. He was weary here – he is beyond weariness there. He was assaulted by the powers of darkness here – he is in unapproachable light there. At the centre of God's glory, he is exalted and empowered. At the centre of the universe is the man of the seamless robe, the carpenter of Nazareth, Mary's child, waiting for the day when in flaming advent glory he will burst forth upon the world as King of kings and Lord of lords – the exalted Messiah.

Not yet do we see the glory of the victory. Not yet do we see all things put under him, but we see Jesus, the man of our humanity, the man touched with the feeling of our infirmity, exalted to the right hand of God. Let us not mistake it in any sense. This one – the child of the Eternal Spirit, the exegesis of God, the firstborn from the dead – is exalted as a Prince and a Saviour and is now at the centre of the universe.

Now the thing to remember is that in the mind and the purpose of God he ever was at the centre. Think of Psalm 24: "Who shall ascend into the hill of the LORD? or who shall stand in his holy place?" (verse 3). That question is soon answered in the psalm: "He that hath clean hands, and a pure heart; who hath not lifted up his soul unto vanity, nor sworn deceitfully" (verse 4). Although the answer came swiftly in the psalm, earth waited spent and restless for the day when the one lonely concentric man would come to an eccentric world and match the perfection which God had revealed in the Psalmist's soul. No man could ascend the hill of the Lord and stand in the holy place in the right of his purity and cleanness and utter integrity – save this one Man of Nazareth. He alone was exalted because of his clean hands and pure heart and because he never once lifted up his soul unto vanity. He is the man in whom there was no cunning, no double-dealing, no guile; a man who dwelt in the realities and became obedient unto death, yea the death of the cross. So the exaltation is of the perfect pattern of human life: wounded, bruised, afflicted, descending and then ascending, and standing in the holy place.

This is the vision of the Holy Spirit in the word of Psalm 24. Thus in the mind of God was the exaltation of the Son before he was born. It can be seen again in Isaiah:

"Look unto me, and be ye saved, all the ends of the earth: for I am God, and there is none else. I have sworn by myself, the word is gone out of my mouth in righteousness, and shall not return, That unto me every knee shall bow, every tongue shall swear."   (45:22,23)

Let us understand that in these words God is speaking geocentrically – as though the earth were a circle and God is at the centre. The expression "the ends of the earth" means the circumference of the earth. God at the centre is speaking to the circumference and to those who move upon it. The idea is confirmed by the meaning of the word "look": "Look unto me ... all the ends of the earth" (verse 22). Literally the Hebrew is 'turn and face unto me' as though from whatever position upon the circumference men may be, if they are to be saved they must turn and face towards the centre – because at the centre is the Saviour.

What constitutes the centre? The answer is in verse 23: "I have sworn by myself, the word is gone out of my mouth in righteousness, and shall not return, That unto me every knee shall bow, every tongue shall swear." You do not have to be a genius to see that Paul has taken these words of Isaiah 45, words which describe the centre of the universe, and has used them to describe the exaltation of the Messiah, the only begotten, in Philippians chapter 2. 'Turn and face unto me all the ends of the earth.' God is saying emphatically that it is only as men do this and associate themselves with the one who is exalted and central, that they have any hope of being saved. He is saying this man alone is acceptable and only those who are his.

"The prince of this world is judged"

There is an interesting allusion to this in the Gospel of John:

"Nevertheless I tell you the truth; It is expedient for you that I go away: for if I go not away, the Comforter will not come unto you; but if I depart, I will send him unto you. And when he is come, he will reprove the world of sin, and of righteousness, and of judgement: of sin, because they believe not on me; of righteousness, because I go to my Father, and ye see me no more; of judgement, because the prince of this world is judged."

(John 16:7-11)

Notice what Jesus is doing here. He is speaking of the testimony of the Holy Spirit to the world. The Holy Spirit was to come – that is to come upon the apostles and by that they would with Spirit inspiration testify to all men the truth about salvation. They would testify of sin; that is, they would reveal a new measurement through which the sin of human hearts would be identified, because of their unbelief.

Then this: "Of righteousness, because I go to my Father". Notice the words "because I go to my Father". That is a reference to the ascension and exaltation of the Son. A new pattern of righteousness has been revealed by the life and death of the Son and because he is able to pass from earth into the very presence of God – "because I go to my Father". It is a signal to all men that this man's righteousness alone is approved. There was nothing to keep him out of heaven. There was no barrier shutting him out from the abode of the invisible God. This is a new ideal of life, a new pattern of living, not written upon stone but upon the heart, able to ennoble the relationship of man with man and make all things new. Thus, "because I go to my Father" is the proof that his exaltation is based upon his purity and perfection.

So to finish the quotation from John: "Of judgement, because the prince of this world is judged". Because of his triumph over sin and because of his consequent exaltation and ascension into heaven, the final judgement of God is pronounced against sin. When God raised him and exalted him, He was saying in the sight of all flesh, 'All men unlike him I reject'. If you say it is severe, you are right: it is severe. God does not parley about gradations of sin. The prince of this world has been judged. When the Messiah rose from death and ascended to heaven the final verdict on sin was formulated and passed and executed. Christ judges the world, proclaims its failure and says that left to itself it is doomed. This is the very essence of the truth which we all believe – that human life, good or bad, is alike not sufficient to save the race. When God said His beloved is the anointed one, He is at the same time saying that the victory over sin which he accomplished is the only source of redemption for sinning men. Those who serve the prince of this world and will not change are doomed and sentenced. The prince of this world is the mastership of this world. Worldliness is revealed in that life which lives as though this were the only world. The life that wilfully is full of everything apart from God, is judged and condemned. Observe then how far-reaching the exaltation of the Messiah really is – in its severity for those who wilfully oppose the purpose of God; in its love and redeeming power for those who are glad to receive him; and in its complete fulfilment of all that God intended when he said, "Let us make man".

Messiah at the centre

This, it seems to me, is in the mind of the Hebrew writer when he wrote the great Hebrew letter:

> "... hath in these last days spoken unto us by his Son, whom he hath appointed heir of all things, by whom also he made the worlds; who being the brightness of his glory, and the express image of his person, and upholding all things by the word of his power, when he had by himself purged our sins, sat down on the right hand of the Majesty on high."   (Hebrews 1:2,3)

It means, as it appears to me, that everything in the universe is set in relation to the Messiah at the centre. When God said, "Let us make man", centrally it was the Messiah He meant. When the Hebrew was pardoned for his sins by the blood of the lamb offered on the altars of Israel, centrally it was the blood of Christ which did it. When God said, "Let there be light", it was Christ which flashed the true light into the universe of God. When God said, "I am ...", centrally it was the Messiah who was to be the perfect and the unique manifestation of the Godhead in the realm of humanity.

Abraham saw his day; Moses bore his reproach; Israel drank of his living water in the wilderness. He is at the centre of all history. All that went before him in time was a preparation for his manifestation. Remember, earth was waiting, spent and restless ... The development of empires, the spread of language, the condition of knowledge – all prepared the world for his coming. All the lines of Hebrew history converge upon him. All the prophecies of Hebrew destiny depend upon him. All the hopes and all the aspirations – all the songs and all the poetry which sighed for salvation have been made incarnate in him. The age-abiding centre of the creation – old and new – the exalted Messiah. What Pilate said sceptically is true essentially: "Behold your King". And let us not miss this point. His exaltation does more than argue his perfection, though it does that wonderfully. More than that, it is the assurance to all of everything that is promised for the future. It is the guarantee of security against all the forces of evil.

Because God has exalted him we know that none can ever dethrone him. And let us face it, they will try, as they always have and as they do now. Say, he is not there; say, he is dead; say, he never existed; say, he is not coming; patronise him; dethrone him at all costs – that is what they say.

Listen to Matthew telling us the word of the anointed one: "All power is given unto me in heaven and in earth." Listen to the promise of the proof:

"Why do the heathen rage, and the people imagine a vain thing? The kings of the earth set themselves, and the rulers take counsel together, against the LORD, and against his anointed, saying, Let us break their bands asunder, and cast away their cords from us." (Psalm 2:1-3)

The answer is your hope:

"Yet have I set my king upon my holy hill of Zion ... Thou art my Son ... Ask of me, and I shall give thee the heathen (nations, RV) for thine inheritance, and the uttermost part of the earth for thy possession." (verses 6-8)

Again: "His enemies shall lick the dust" (Psalm 72:9). The greatest enemy of all he met face to face and front to front, met it, defied it and defeated it. The prince of this world was beaten in a fair fight. So the victor broke the bars of death asunder, and went his shining way into the presence of the Eternal Spirit, the Father. He is exalted. Heaven recognises it; earth knows it, and because of it every knee shall bow and every tongue shall confess that Jesus Christ is Lord, to the glory of God the Father. We thank God that He has raised up a horn of salvation in the house of His servant David. We thank God that he is coming soon – Matthew's Messiah. From him all light is streaming and all songs are coming and all hope is flaming. Across the fret and fever of the world he will cast the infinite peace of God. There is cause for joy. As you come to the close of our brief consideration of Matthew's Messiah, you have reason to go in peace, with a lilt in your step and with a song in your heart. God grant you may feel it to be true.

Scripture index